MACMILLAN READERS

UPPER LEVEL

CHARLES DICKENS

Great Expectations

Retold by Florence Bell

Macmillan Readers is a series of engaging narrative texts designed to stimulate learners while enhancing their language skills, building literacy and boosting reading confidence. Through captivating stories and fascinating cultural themes, learners will explore a diversity of scenarios that foster vocabulary expansion, comprehension skills and a lifelong love of reading.

The right reader at every stage
Tailored to each learner's stage of language proficiency, our six levels feature text adapted to match the skill level. With controlled vocabulary and grammar, learners can read freely and immerse themselves in the story. When more challenging words are introduced, either the text will provide sufficient context to aid understanding or a full explanation will be provided in the Glossary.

Readers for all, anywhere, anytime
Macmillan Readers are perfect for shared, guided and independent reading. Whether in traditional print, immersive audio or the convenient eBook, Macmillan Readers are equally effective for in-class activities, paired discussions or solo reading at home or on the move.

Reading for pleasure, knowledge and well-being
Regular reading and reading for pleasure:
- increases reading confidence, benefiting all literacy skills, not just reading.
- reinforces and enriches vocabulary, providing a variety of contexts.
- expands general knowledge.
- supports concentration, inner reflection and well-being.

Macmillan Readers will inspire a love for reading in English while nurturing essential language skills. Unlock new worlds, expand horizons and embark on an adventure in English!

(NOTE: While the content of Macmillan Readers is evaluated for age suitability, we kindly remind parents and teachers that they are ultimately responsible for determining whether a particular book is appropriate for their child or student.)

Contents

	The People in This Story	*4*
	A Note About the Author	*5*
	A Note About England in the Nineteenth Century	*6*
1	In the Churchyard	*8*
2	Christmas Day	*15*
3	At Miss Havisham's	*19*
4	The Pale Young Gentleman	*27*
5	'I Must Become a Gentleman!'	*31*
6	Great Expectations	*34*
7	Learning to be a Gentleman	*39*
8	Young Men in Love	*47*
9	I Come of Age	*51*
10	Abel Magwitch	*58*
11	Secrets from the Past	*66*
12	Escape	*74*
13	Friends Together	*78*
	Points for Understanding	*84*
	Glossary	*89*
	1 Terms to do with blacksmiths and blacksmithing	*89*
	2 Terms to do with criminals, lawyers and the law	
	in nineteenth century England	*89*
	3 Adjectives and adverbs	*90*
	4 Special language in this story	*91*
	5 General	*92*

The People in This Story

Wemmick   Mr Jaggers

The Convict

A Note About the Author

Charles Dickens is one of the greatest writers in the English language. He was born near Portsmouth in the south of England on 7th February 1812. His father worked in an office as a clerk.

Charles Dickens' father was not clever at managing money. John Dickens did not earn much money and soon the family could not pay their bills. John Dickens went to prison because he could not pay his debts. Mrs Dickens, Charles and his brothers and sisters went to live in the prison with Charles' father. At this time, Charles Dickens was 12 years old. He was sent to work in a factory. He had to work many hours a day sticking labels on bottles. The pay was low, the work was very hard and Dickens was very unhappy. Charles Dickens never forgot what happened to him at this time.

In 1827, when he was 15 years old, Dickens went to work in an

A Note About the Author

office as a clerk. The work was not well-paid but Charles made some friends and also liked visiting the theatre.

In 1833, Dickens started writing. That year, his first article was published in the *Old Monthly Magazine*.

Charles Dickens became very famous and very rich. He wrote some of the most well-known and popular stories in English literature. Dickens knew how the poor people lived in England and many of his stories were about poor people. He was angry at the way children were treated. They were beaten and made to work in dirty and dangerous jobs with little food or shelter. Because of his stories, people were made to see how children and poor people lived in nineteenth century England.

Dickens wrote a very great number of books, articles and short stories. He owned and edited magazines which published short stories and poetry. He also travelled in Europe and the United States. Thousands of people came to hear him talk and to hear him read from his books.

Oliver Twist, the story of a poor boy without a family, was published in 1838. Other well-known books by Dickens are: *A Christmas Carol* (1843), *Bleak House* (1853), *A Tale of Two Cities* (1859), *Great Expectations* (1861), and *Our Mutual Friend* (1865).

Charles Dickens became ill from working too hard and died on 9th June 1870 near Gravesend in the south of England. He was 58 years old. Dickens was buried in the famous church, Westminster Abbey, in London.

A Note About England in the Nineteenth Century

Dickens' story, *Great Expectations*, is set between the years 1810 and 1830. The story takes place in London and in the county of Kent in the south-east of England. Dickens knew both of these parts of England very well.

A Note About England in the Nineteenth Century

Great Britain became very wealthy in the middle of the nineteenth century. London was the largest city in Europe and many people suddenly became rich. People who had money could become part of Society. Society people were known as ladies and gentlemen. These people were educated. They visited one another's houses and went to dinners, parties and dances. They lived in fine houses and had servants.

The people in Society made rules for correct behaviour and correct dress. To be dressed according to these rules was to be dressed well, in the most fashionable clothes.

However, most people in England at this time did not have much money. They could not become ladies and gentlemen. Thousands of poor people in London lived in small, dirty houses and did not have enough to eat. They had no work and many men, women and children became criminals.

When he lived in London, Dickens saw the rich people living in expensive houses and he also saw the dark and narrow streets nearby where the poor people lived and died.

When he was a boy, Charles Dickens had lived near the marshes between the River Medway and the River Thames in Kent. This part of south-east England is very flat and wet. There are many rivers and ditches full of water and the sea is not far away.

The people who lived on the marshes at this time were poor and their lives were hard. Many of them were farmers or labourers. The people had very little education.

There were no cars, trains or telephones at this time. People travelled in coaches pulled by horses. Letters were carried in these coaches too. London is 26 miles away from this part of Kent but the roads were bad in the nineteenth century and the journey from the marshes to London took many hours.

Most of the poor people living on the marshes did not visit London by coach. They did not know anything about the lives of the rich people living in London. They stayed on their farms and in their small shops. They worked hard to earn a little money.

1
In the Churchyard

My name is Philip Pirrip, but as a child I could not say my name. I called myself Pip, and that has been my name ever since.

I never knew my mother and father. They both died when I was a baby. I was brought up by my only sister, who was married to a blacksmith[1], Joe Gargery.

My story begins on a cold, grey winter afternoon in the churchyard where my parents are buried. I would often go to their graves and look down at the words on their gravestone: *Philip Pirrip and Georgiana, Wife of the Above*. I was a sensitive and lonely child and was often sad.

The marshes beyond the churchyard were grey. The river beyond the marshes was a darker line of grey. A bitter[3] wind was blowing across the marshes from the sea. The graveyard was a dark and frightening place.

I shivered. Cold and afraid, I began to cry.

'Quiet, you little devil[4]!' cried a terrible voice. 'Keep still – or I'll cut your throat!'

A rough-looking man had taken hold of me. He held me tightly by the neck.

'Oh, don't cut my throat, sir!' I cried. 'Please, don't!'

The man's rough grey clothes were torn and muddy[3]. Like me, he was shivering with cold. His shoes were old and broken. He had a torn piece of cloth tied round his head. And his eyes were wild and terrible.

'Tell me your name,' the man growled[5]. 'Tell me. Quick!'

'Pip, sir. Pip,' I answered.

'Show me where you live,' the terrible man demanded.

In the Churchyard

I pointed towards our village, which was about a mile away from the churchyard.

The man stared at me for a moment. Then, with a sudden movement, he picked me up and turned me upside down[5]. A piece of bread fell out of my pocket. The man pushed me onto a gravestone. Then he grabbed the bread and began eating greedily.

I sat on the gravestone where he had put me, shivering and crying with fear.

'Now, tell me, where's your mother?' the man in grey asked suddenly.

'There, sir,' I answered, pointing over his shoulder to my mother's grave.

The man looked behind him and started to run.

'I mean – she's buried there, sir. That's my mother. "Georgiana, Wife of the Above".'

'Oh, I see,' the man said, limping[5] slowly back. 'And is that your father there buried with your mother?'

'Yes, sir,' I replied.

'Then who do you live with?' the man asked. 'That is, if I let you live,' he said roughly.

'With my sister, sir – Mrs Joe Gargery – wife of Joe Gargery, the blacksmith, sir.'

'A blacksmith, is he?' the man muttered[5], looking down at his leg. There was a thick band of iron round his ankle, with a broken chain hanging from the band.

The man came nearer. He took hold of my arms and tipped me back over the gravestone as far as I could go. His terrible eyes stared into mine.

'Now, look here[4],' he said. 'Do you know what a file[1] is?'

'Yes, sir.'

'Then you get me a file. And you get me some food. Do you understand?'

'Yes, sir.'

'Bring me, early tomorrow morning, a file and some food,' the

He took hold of my arms and tipped me back over the gravestone as far as I could go. His terrible eyes stared into mine.

In the Churchyard

man repeated slowly. 'Bring them to the Old Fort[5], over there, by the river. Say nothing to no one and maybe I'll let you live.

'But if you tell anyone about me,' the terrible man said slowly, 'your heart and liver will be torn out! Torn out, roasted and ate[4].

'Now, I'm not alone,' he went on. 'There's a young man near here, listening to every word I say. He has a secret way of finding a boy, wherever he is. Even if a boy is warm in bed, behind a locked door, that young man will find him. What do you say to that?'

I promised I would bring him the file and the food very early in the morning.

'Lord strike me dead if I don't[4] – say it!' the man growled. 'Lord strike me dead if I don't,' I repeated.

The man lifted me down from the gravestone. Then he held his arms around his shivering body.

'Goodnight, sir,' I whispered.

'Nothing much good about it,' the man replied, looking across at wet and windy marshes. 'I wish I was a frog – or a fish!'

He limped off through the churchyard, towards the marshes. He turned once to look back at me.

I began to run home as fast as I could.

When I got home, the forge[1] was shut up. Joe had finished work for the day. I opened the door of the house. I crept quietly into the warm kitchen and saw Joe, sitting alone by the fire, smoking his pipe.

Joe Gargery was a huge, fair haired man with kind blue eyes. He looked at me sadly.

'Mrs Joe has been out looking for you, Pip,' Joe told me. 'She's out there now, Pip. And she's got Tickler with her.'

This was very bad news. Tickler was a stick that I had often felt on my thin body.

For although I had food, clothes and shelter, my sister was a hard and angry woman and would often beat me. Her husband, Joe, was my only friend.

In the Churchyard

'Has she been out long, Joe?' I asked nervously.

'Well,' said Joe, looking up at the clock, 'this time, she's been out about five minutes.

'And I hear her coming back, Pip old chap[4],' Joe added. 'Get behind the door!'

My sister pushed open the door with a bang. She soon saw where I was hiding and beat me until I cried. Then she threw me angrily across the kitchen to where Joe was sitting. Joe quietly placed me in the corner near the fire and protected me with his own powerful body.

My sister was twenty years older than me. She was tall and thin, with a hard face and sharp black eyes. The rough red skin on her bony hands and face made her always look angry.

'Where have you been, you young monkey?' Mrs Joe cried, stamping her foot. 'Tell me what you've been doing all this time!'

'I've been in the churchyard,' I answered, crying.

'Churchyard?' Mrs Joe repeated sharply. 'You'd have been in the churchyard long ago, if it hadn't been for me[4]. Who brought you up? Tell me that!'

'You did,' I sobbed.

'And why I did, I don't know,' my sister exclaimed. 'It's bad enough looking after this blacksmith, without being your mother too! One of these days, you'll drive me to the graveyard, the pair of you.'

Joe said nothing. He was a simple, gentle man and he never complained about Mrs Joe's bad temper. But he protected me when he could and I loved him for it.

It was Christmas Eve and Mrs Joe was very busy. She was making the food for the Christmas meal next day. She made me stir the mixture for the Christmas pudding for an hour and then I was allowed to sit by the fire with Joe.

As I sat by the warm fire, I thought of the man on the cold, wet marshes. I remembered my promise to him. I thought of the young man who would find me and kill me if I broke that promise.

12

In the Churchyard

The silence of the quiet night was suddenly broken by loud noises that seemed to come from the sea.

'Are those the great guns, Joe?' I asked.

Joe nodded.

'Another convict's[2] escaped,' he said. 'One got away last night and the guns were fired for him. Now they're giving warning that a second one has escaped.'

'Who's firing the guns?' I asked.

'Ask no questions and you'll be told no lies[4],' my sister snapped in reply.

'Mrs Joe,' I said politely, 'I really should like to know, if you don't mind, where the firing comes from.'

'From the Hulks[2], the Hulks,' my sister answered.

'And, please, what are the Hulks?'

'Hulks are prison ships, moored[5] on the other side of the marshes,' Mrs Joe explained impatiently.

'I wonder who's put into prison ships and why they're put there,' I said.

Mrs Joe leapt up and grabbed me by the ear.

'People are put in the Hulks because they murder and rob and do all kinds of bad things,' she said. 'And they all begin by asking questions!'

Mrs Joe pulled my ear hard as she spoke and gave me a push.

'And now go off to bed!' she added.

I went slowly up the dark stairs, thinking about the terrible prison ships. I had begun by asking questions. And, in a few hours, I was going to steal from Mrs Joe!

I slept very little that night. I was afraid of Mrs Joe. I was afraid of the convict on the marshes. And, most of all, I was afraid of the terrible young man.

———

At last, the grey light of dawn came into the sky. I got up and dressed. Quietly and carefully, I crept downstairs to the pantry.

I found some bread, a piece of cheese and a large bone with some

In the Churchyard

meat on it. There was a bottle with a little brandy in it and I took that too. Last of all, on the top shelf, I found a beautiful, round meat pie.

A door in the kitchen led into the forge. I unlocked the door and looked for a file among Joe's tools. Then, locking the door behind me, I walked back through the kitchen.

Turning the big key, I opened the house door carefully. In a few moments, I was running as fast as I could towards the Fort on the misty[3] marshes.

It was a frosty[3] morning and very damp and cold. The grass was wet and water dripped from the trees. The mist was so thick over the marshes that I could only see a few feet ahead of me. As I ran, trees, cows and gates seemed to lean out of the mist to stop me.

I knew the Fort well, but in my terror, I almost lost my way. I had just crossed a ditch[5] when I saw the man in grey. He was sitting on the ground with his back to me. I walked up to him quietly and touched his shoulder. He jumped up and turned to face me. It was not the same man!

But he was dressed in the same rough clothes as the man I had met. He too had an iron on his leg. It was the young man, waiting to tear my heart and liver out!

With a cry, I ran on until I had reached the Fort. And there was my convict. He was swinging his arms and walking up and down to keep warm.

The man grabbed the food from my hand and began eating in great mouthfuls like a dog. When he drank the brandy, he shivered so violently that his teeth nearly broke the bottle.

As he started to eat the pie, I spoke to him.

'I'm glad you're enjoying it, sir,' I said.

'Thank you, my boy. I am, I am,' he replied.

'Aren't you leaving anything for him?' I asked anxiously.

'Him? Oh, the young man. He doesn't need any food,' the convict replied.

'Doesn't he? I thought he looked hungry,' I said.

'Looked? When did you see him?'

'Just now,' I answered.

'Where?'

'Over there,' I said, pointing. 'I thought he was you,' I explained.

The man stopped eating and grabbed my jacket.

'What did the man look like?' he asked me fiercely.

'He... he was dressed like you and... he had an iron on his leg,' I answered. 'And there was a long scar on his face.'

'Was there?' the convict cried. 'So he's escaped from the Hulks, has he? I thought I heard the guns last night. Where is he? I must find him. Curse this iron on my leg[4]. Give me that file, boy. And tell me where you saw him.'

I pointed to where I had seen the young man. The convict stared through the mist. Then, sitting down on the wet grass, he began to file at the heavy iron on his leg.

The sky was lighter now and I dared not stay any longer. My sister and Joe would soon be awake. They would be looking for me. I began to walk quietly away.

When I looked back, the convict was bent over, filing at the iron on his leg. When I looked back again, I could see nothing through the thick mist. But I could still hear the sound of the file as it cut through the heavy leg-iron.

2

Christmas Day

When I got home, Mrs Joe was too busy preparing our Christmas dinner to ask me questions. I sat down quietly by Joe.

Our dinner was to be at half past one. Long before that, I was scrubbed clean by Mrs Joe and dressed in my best clothes. It was my job to open the door to our guests – three of our neighbours, and Uncle Pumblechook.

Christmas Day

Uncle Pumblechook was a fat, stupid man with hair that stood up on his head. He greatly admired[5] my sister but thought very little of Joe and myself. He had brought two bottles of wine and he gave them to Mrs Joe with a bow[5] and a smile.

Everyone was soon eating and drinking happily. Everyone except me. I was terrified. Was Mrs Joe going to serve the pie today? When would she discover it was missing?

Dinner seemed to be finished, when my sister suddenly spoke to Joe.

'Fetch clean plates!' she ordered. I held on tight to the table leg. I knew what was going to happen.

My sister smiled at her guests.

'And now you must all taste another gift from Uncle Pumblechook,' she said. 'It's a delicious meat pie!'

'Well, Mrs Joe, this has been a wonderful meal,' Uncle Pumblechook said happily. 'But I think I could eat a slice of that meat pie!'

My sister hurried into the pantry and Uncle Pumblechook picked up his knife and fork.

'You shall have a slice of pie, Pip,' Joe whispered to me.

I could not sit there any longer. Did I cry out or not? I can't remember. But I jumped up and ran towards the front door. At the same moment, Mrs Joe came back from the pantry.

'What's happened to the meat pie?' she cried.

I opened the door and ran – straight into a group of soldiers. Their leader, a sergeant, was holding out a pair of handcuffs[2]!

'Now then, young man!' the sergeant said sharply, as he marched into our kitchen.

'Excuse me, ladies and gentlemen,' he went on. 'We're chasing escaped convicts and we need the blacksmith.'

'What do you want him for?' my sister asked in surprise.

'Well I'd like to stay and talk to his charming wife,' the sergeant replied. 'But today we're busy with the King's business. We need the blacksmith to do a little job for us.'

Christmas Day

Joe stood up and the sergeant held out the handcuffs.

'There's something wrong with these, blacksmith,' the sergeant said. 'We need them today, so I'd like you to mend them.'

Joe took the handcuffs in his great hand.

'I'll have to light the fire in the forge,' he said. 'This job will take about two hours.'

'That'll be all right,' the sergeant answered. 'We're sure that the convicts are still on the marshes. We'll capture them before it's dark. No one has seen them, I suppose?'

Everyone except me shook their heads. No one thought of asking me.

Joe took off his coat and got ready for work. With the soldiers' help, the forge fire was soon burning fiercely. As Joe hammered the white-hot iron, we all stood round and watched him.

Mrs Joe gave the soldiers some beer. Uncle Pumblechook poured out wine for the sergeant and then poured some for everyone else. Even I got a little wine.

We stood in the forge, laughing and talking. I thought sadly of the two convicts, cold and hungry on the marshes.

At last the handcuffs were mended. Joe asked the sergeant if he could follow the soldiers while they searched for the convicts.

'Certainly, blacksmith. Bring the boy with you, if you like,' the sergeant answered.

'Well,' my sister said sharply, 'if he gets his head shot off, don't ask me to mend it.'

Joe lifted me up onto his broad shoulders. As we began to follow the soldiers, I whispered in his ear.

'I hope, Joe, that we don't find them!'

And Joe whispered back. 'Let's hope they've got away, Pip old chap.'

It was dark now. On our way to the marshes, the bitter wind blew icy[3] rain into our faces.

The group of soldiers moved quickly. We went at a fast pace, sometimes stumbling on the rough ground, sometimes falling. At last

17

we were on the marshes, splashing in and out of the ditches full of icy water.

Suddenly, we heard a shout. We stopped and listened. The shout was repeated and then we heard another.

The sergeant sent us to the right. On we ran, even faster, splashing through ditches, up and down steep banks.

And now we could hear that two men were shouting.

'Murder!' one cried.

'Convicts! This way for the escaped convicts!' shouted the other.

The two men were fighting at the bottom of a ditch. They were splashing in the muddy water. The men were cursing and hitting out at each other.

When the soldiers pulled the men from the ditch, both of the convicts were torn and bleeding.

My convict wiped the blood from his face with his torn sleeve.

'I caught this man! I'm giving him to you!' he cried. 'Don't forget that. I caught him for you!'

'That won't help you,' the sergeant answered, as the two convicts were handcuffed.

'I don't expect it to help me. I caught him and that's enough for me,' my convict answered.

The other convict's clothes were torn and his face was bloody. But I could still see the scar on his cheek.

'He tried to murder me, sergeant!' the young man said.

'Tried?' my convict repeated. 'Do you think I would try and not succeed? No, I caught him and held him here. I could have escaped, but I wouldn't let this gentleman get away. He tricked me once. I'll not let him trick me again!'

'He tried to murder me,' the other man repeated weakly.

'He's lying. He always was a liar,' my convict answered. 'We were put on trial[2] together and he lied at the trial. He was scared of me then and he's scared of me now. Look at him! Look at the gentleman convict, shaking with fear!'

'That's enough!' the sergeant said. 'Light the torches there!' he shouted to the soldiers.

It was very dark now. There was no moon. In the light of the torches, my convict turned and saw me for the first time.

'Wait a minute,' my convict said to the sergeant. 'I wish to say something. I don't want anyone to be blamed for what I did. A man must eat. I took drink and food from the village. I took bread, cheese, brandy and a meat pie. From the blacksmith's house.'

'Has a pie been stolen from you?' the sergeant asked Joe.

'Yes, my wife found out it was missing – at the very moment you came in,' Joe answered. 'That's right, isn't it, Pip?'

'Then I'm very sorry I ate your pie, blacksmith,' the convict said, not looking at me.

'You're welcome to it, poor miserable fellow,' Joe said kindly. 'We don't know what you've done, but we wouldn't want you to starve, would we, Pip?'

The convict wiped his torn sleeve across his eyes and turned away. Joe and I watched as the two men were led away towards the sea and the prison ships.

Days later, when I saw Joe looking for his file in the forge, I nearly told him the truth. But I was a coward and too afraid of what he would think of me.

3

At Miss Havisham's

One evening, about two years later, Joe and I were sitting together by the fire. Mrs Joe had gone to town with Uncle Pumblechook in the pony cart[5].

I had learnt to read and write a little and Joe was very proud of me. I was trying to teach him the alphabet. But the only letters he could recognize were J, O, and E.

'We don't know what you've done, but we wouldn't want you to starve, would we, Pip?' said Joe.

At Miss Havisham's

'I think it's too late for me to learn, Pip old chap,' Joe said sadly. 'I never went to school. My mother wanted me to go to school but my father would not let me. He was a hard man, Pip. My father was a blacksmith. He kept me away from school and made me work for him. He was cruel to my mother and often beat her.

'That's why I let your sister do what she wants,' Joe explained. 'She's hard on you, I know, Pip, but she has a good heart. She looked after you when your mother and father died. She was looking after you when she agreed to marry me. "Bring the poor little child", I told her. "There's room at the forge for him." '

I began to cry and to thank Joe for his kindness. I knew what a good friend he was to me.

It was now eight o'clock and dark outside. Joe put more coal on the fire. We stood by the door and listened for the sound of Uncle Pumblechook's pony cart.

Not long afterwards, my sister and Uncle Pumblechook arrived. They stood and warmed themselves by our kitchen fire. As Mrs Joe took off her bonnet and shawl, she looked at me sharply.

'Well, this boy should be grateful to me now,' she cried.

Joe and I looked at each other in surprise.

'Quite right, quite right,' Uncle Pumblechook replied. 'He should be grateful for the opportunity she's giving him!'

Joe and I were even more surprised.

'Well, what are you staring at?' Mrs Joe snapped. Her face was redder than ever with the cold.

'A "she" was mentioned . . .' Joe began politely.

'Miss Havisham isn't a "he", I suppose,' my sister answered sharply.

'Miss Havisham who lives in town?' Joe asked in surprise. 'How does Miss Havisham know Pip? She never leaves her house, does she?'

'She doesn't know Pip, but she does know Uncle Pumblechook,' Mrs Joe explained impatiently. 'She wants a boy to go to her house and play. Uncle Pumblechook kindly mentioned this boy here. So

At Miss Havisham's

he's going back to town with Uncle Pumblechook tonight. And tomorrow he'll play at Miss Havisham's, or I'll play[4] with him!'

Without another word, Mrs Joe grabbed hold of me with her bony hands. She washed and scrubbed me until I could hardly breathe. Then I was dressed in my best clothes and given to Uncle Pumblechook.

'Goodbye, Joe!' I cried, as I was pushed out of the door by Mrs Joe.

'Goodbye and God bless you[4], Pip old chap!' Joe answered. In a moment, I was sitting in Uncle Pumblechook's pony cart and we were on our way to town.

At ten o'clock the next morning, Uncle Pumblechook drove me to Satis House where Miss Havisham lived.

The house was very big and gloomy[3]. The tall iron gates in front of the house were locked. Uncle Pumblechook rang the bell and we waited.

In a few minutes, a beautifully dressed girl came across the paved courtyard towards us. She was very pretty and she looked very proud.

'What name?' the young lady asked.

'Pumblechook. And this is Pip,' Uncle Pumblechook answered politely.

'This is Pip, is it?' the girl said, looking at me scornfully[3]. 'Come in, Pip.'

The girl was carrying a large bunch of keys. She unlocked the gate with one of them and held the gate open. I went in and Uncle Pumblechook started to follow. But the girl stopped him.

'Do you wish to see Miss Havisham?' she asked.

'If Miss Havisham wishes to see me . . .' Uncle Pumblechook began.

'But she doesn't,' the girl said sharply. 'Come along, boy.'

She locked the gate and led me across the courtyard. It was clean, but grass grew between the stones, as though no one ever walked there. I saw now that the girl was about my age. But she was so beautiful and so proud that she seemed much older.

The big front door had chains across it. We walked on to a side door and the girl opened it.

Inside the house everything was dark. The curtains were drawn and the shutters were closed on all the windows. The girl picked up a burning candle and this was our only light. She led me along several dark passages and up a wide staircase. At last, we came to a door where the girl stopped.

'Go in,' she said.

'After you, miss,' I whispered politely.

'Don't be silly, I'm not going in!' the girl answered. And she walked away, taking the candle with her.

Feeling very afraid, I knocked at the door.

'Come in,' a woman's voice said quietly.

I opened the door slowly and went inside. I looked around me in the greatest surprise.

The room was large and full of furniture. But heavy curtains shut out the daylight and the room was lit only by candles. I saw that I was in a lady's dressing room[5]. And at the dressing table sat the strangest lady I had ever seen.

She was dressed richly, in satin and lace clothes, and everything she wore was white. A long white wedding veil[5] hung down from her head. I saw with surprise that the lady's hair was white, too. She wore bright jewels and there were other jewels lying on the table in front of her. One of her shoes lay on the floor. The other one was lying on the dressing table. Her elbow was on the dressing table and she was resting her face on her hand.

Trunks full of clothes were placed about the room. Each one contained many silk and satin dresses. But the dresses were faded[3] and torn.

And then I saw that everything that had once been white was now faded and yellow. The fair young bride was now an old woman

At Miss Havisham's

whose skin was yellow and wrinkled. Only her dark eyes showed that she was alive.

Then the lady moved and those dark eyes stared at me.

'Who is it?' she asked

'Pip, ma'am[4]. Mr Pumblechook's boy. I've come to play.'

'Come here. Let me look at you,' the lady said.

I moved nearer, but I was afraid to look at her. Then I saw that a watch on the dressing table had stopped at twenty to nine.

'Are you afraid to look at me?' the lady asked me slowly. 'Are you afraid to look at a woman who hasn't seen the sun shine since before you were born?

'Look here,' Miss Havisham whispered, touching her heart. 'My heart is broken[4], broken. And I am so tired . . . But I thought I would like to see a child play . . . So play, boy, play!'

I stood there, unable to move, not knowing what to do.

'Call Estella,' Miss Havisham said at last. 'Go to the door and call her.'

I was afraid, but I had to do what she asked. So I opened the door. I called out several times, then I saw the girl walking towards me, the candle in her hand.

Miss Havisham smiled as the beautiful girl came into the room. She held a jewel against Estella's pretty brown hair.

'My jewels will be yours one day,' Miss Havisham said quietly. 'Now I want you to play cards with this boy.'

'This boy? But he's so common[5]!' Estella exclaimed. 'Look at his clothes. He's just a common working boy!'

'Never mind,' Miss Havisham whispered. 'You can break his heart, can't you?'

So I played cards with Estella. When I made mistakes, she laughed at me and so, of course, I made more.

'What rough hands this boy has!' Estella exclaimed, as I held the cards. 'And what heavy boots he's wearing!'

'Why don't you answer her, Pip?' Miss Havisham said at last. 'She says cruel things about you. What do you think of her?'

'What rough hands this boy has!' Estella exclaimed, as I held the cards. 'And what heavy boots he's wearing!'

At Miss Havisham's

'I don't want to say,' I replied.

'Whisper to me,' Miss Havisham said, bending down.

'I think she is very proud,' I said quietly.

'Yes, and what else?'

'I think she is very pretty,' I went on.

'Anything else?'

'I think she is very rude. And please,' I added, 'I should like to go home now.'

'Finish your game of cards first,' Miss Havisham said.

When Estella had won the last game, she threw the cards down with a scornful smile.

'Come here again in six days, Pip,' Miss Havisham said as I was leaving. 'Take him downstairs, Estella. Give him something to eat and drink before he goes.'

I followed Estella down the gloomy stairs and along the dark corridors. She opened the side door and the bright daylight hurt my eyes and confused me.

Estella told me to wait in the courtyard. In a few minutes, she returned with some meat and bread. She placed the food on the ground, as though I was a dog. Tears came into my eyes. I turned my head away, so that Estella would not see me crying. But when she had gone, I cried aloud and kicked the wall with the heavy boots she had laughed at.

After a time, Estella returned with her keys and unlocked the iron gate.

'Why aren't you crying?' she asked me with a smile.

'Because I don't want to,' I replied.

'Yes, you do,' she said. 'Your eyes are red with crying. You are nearly crying now.'

She laughed, pushed me outside the gate and locked it behind me.

I went straight back to Uncle Pumblechook's, but he was not at home. So I began the long walk back to the forge alone.

As I walked along, I thought about the strange things I had seen.

I thought of Estella and her scorn. She had made me ashamed of my clothes, my boots and most of all, myself. I wished I had never seen her. But then I remembered how beautiful she was.

4

The Pale Young Gentleman

When I got home, my sister made me sit on a stool and began asking me questions.

'Tell me what Miss Havisham looks like,' my sister demanded. 'What did she say to you? What did you do?'

'Miss Havisham's very tall and dark,' I answered quickly. 'She was sitting in a black velvet coach. There was a girl with her. She gave us cake on gold plates!'

'Gold plates!' Mrs Joe repeated slowly. Then she added, 'I hope you pleased her. She wanted you to play. Did you?'

'Oh, yes. We played with . . . with flags[5],' I said. 'And then we shouted and waved our swords!'

'Swords?'

'Yes. The girl – Estella – got them from a cupboard. And there was no daylight in the room, only candles!'

Joe's eyes opened very wide.

Why was I telling all these lies? I do not know. Perhaps the truth was too strange. My visit to Miss Havisham had confused and frightened me.

And Estella's words had hurt me. She had called me a common working boy. What would she think of Joe? How heavy his boots were!

The following week, I walked to Miss Havisham's alone. As before, Estella unlocked the gate and took me into the house.

The Pale Young Gentleman

'Am I pretty?' she said suddenly, holding up the candle.

'Yes, very pretty,' I answered.

'Am I rude?'

'Not so rude as last time.'

'Not so rude?' Estella repeated angrily. And she slapped my face hard.

'What do you think now?' she asked.

'I won't tell you,' I said.

'Then why don't you cry, you horrid, common boy?'

'I'm not crying. I'll never cry for you again!' I answered. But I was crying as I spoke. And, God knows, I cried for Estella many, many times afterwards.

As we were going upstairs, we passed a tall man with sharp eyes and thick black eyebrows. His large hands were very clean and white.

'Who's this?' the man asked, staring at me.

'Only a boy,' Estella answered.

The man held my chin in his hand and stared into my eyes.

'Why are you here?' he asked.

'Miss Havisham asked me to come,' I whispered.

'Did she? Then behave yourself!' the man said, as he went on down the stairs.

Miss Havisham was sitting in her dressing room. She was wearing the same torn dress as before. Everything in the room was the same.

'So you're back again,' Miss Havisham said. 'Are you ready to play today?'

I was too frightened to answer.

'Well, if you can't play, can you work?' Miss Havisham asked.

'Yes, ma'am.'

'Then go into the room on the other side of the corridor. Wait there till I come.'

The room I entered was very big. In the middle of the room was a long table. By the light of the fire and the many candles, I saw that the torn tablecloth was covered with dust.

The Pale Young Gentleman

There was something tall and white on the table too. It was covered with dust and fat black spiders were running all over it.

Miss Havisham came into the room and stood behind me. She placed her hand on my shoulder and pointed at the table with a walking stick.

'Look, Pip,' she said. 'Can you see my wedding cake? Eaten by mice and spiders. Ruined!'

Miss Havisham held my shoulder hard with her thin hand.

'Help me walk, Pip,' she said.

We walked slowly round and round the long table, the strange old lady leaning on my shoulder.

'Today is my birthday, Pip,' Miss Havisham said. 'Many years ago, it should have been my wedding day. The dress I am wearing now was new then and I was young. Everything is old and ruined now. Time has ruined me too and broken my heart.'

What could I say? We stood there, very quiet, in the candlelight.

'Call Estella,' Miss Havisham said at last. 'Play with her again. I want to see her beat you at cards again!'

So Estella and I played cards. She won every game. Miss Havisham smiled and held bright jewels against Estella's hair. How beautiful the proud girl looked!

Miss Havisham was soon tired and I was sent downstairs. When I had eaten, I walked sadly through the courtyard and into an overgrown garden. No one had looked after the garden for years. Weeds grew everywhere.

Turning a corner, I came face to face with a fair-haired boy of my own age.

'Hello,' said this pale young gentleman. 'Who let you in?'

'Miss Estella,' I answered.

'Oh, did she? Then let's fight!'

I stared at the boy in surprise. Then, suddenly, he pulled my hair and hit me hard in the stomach with his head.

I was so surprised, that I hit him hard.

'So you do want to fight, do you?' the pale young gentleman

The Pale Young Gentleman

cried. 'Come on, then!' Then he raised his fists like a boxer and began waving them in front of my face.

I hit him again and he fell backwards onto the ground. When he got up, his nose was bleeding. A minute later, I had hit him in the eye.

'You've won,' he said weakly. 'Shake hands.'

So we shook hands and the young gentleman walked quietly away.

Estella was waiting for me at the gate. Her eyes were bright and shining. I knew she had been watching the fight.

'You can kiss me if you like,' she said.

I was confused but happy. I kissed her gently on the cheek. A few minutes later, I began my long walk home.

From that day onwards, I visited Miss Havisham three times a week. I did not see the pale young gentleman again, but Estella was always there.

On every visit, I pushed Miss Havisham round and round those two rooms in a wheelchair. She did not walk with me again. Instead I pushed her in her chair. As I walked behind her, Miss Havisham questioned me. I told her I was going to be apprenticed[1] to Joe, when I was old enough. I told her that I knew nothing, but wanted to know everything. I told her I wanted to be educated. I told her how I wanted to be a gentleman. Perhaps I hoped that Miss Havisham would pay for my education. But she never suggested it.

Sometimes Estella was kind to me, but, more often, she was rude and cruel. I could not understand this proud, beautiful girl who made me so unhappy.

5
'I Must Become a Gentleman!'

My life went on without change for two or three years. One day Miss Havisham looked up at me, and said, 'You are getting tall, Pip. What is the name of your brother-in-law, the blacksmith?'

'Joe Gargery, ma'am,' I answered.

'It is time for you to be apprenticed to him,' Miss Havisham said. 'Bring him with you one day. Bring him soon!'

So, two days later, Joe put on his Sunday clothes and boots. Looking very awkward and uncomfortable, he walked with me to Satis House, where Miss Havisham lived.

Estella opened the gate for us. She smiled scornfully at Joe and I felt ashamed of him.

Joe was so afraid of Miss Havisham that he refused to look at her. He stood near the door, turning his hat round and round in his strong hands.

Miss Havisham picked up a little bag from her dressing table. She held it out to Joe.

'It is time Pip became your apprentice,' she said. 'Pip has earned his premium[1] and here it is.

'There are twenty-five guineas in this bag, Pip,' she said to me. 'Give them to Joe Gargery. He is your master now. Goodbye.'

And she turned away.

I looked at Miss Havisham and Estella in despair.

'But don't you want me to come again, Miss Havisham?' I asked.

'No, Pip. Gargery is your master and you must work for him.

'Pip has been a good boy here,' Miss Havisham said to Joe. 'This money is his reward. You are an honest man and will not expect more. Let them out, Estella.'

Bitterly[3] disappointed, I led Joe from that strange room. He walked like a man in a dream.

'I Must Become a Gentleman!'

And so I became a blacksmith. From that day, I lived in fear. Fear that Estella might see me at work with my dirty face and dirty hands. In my mind, I saw her beautiful face, with its hard, scornful smile.

A year passed. I still thought about Estella every day. I longed to see Estella again. So I decided to go to Satis House. I asked Joe for a holiday and he agreed to close the forge for a day.

When I reached Satis House, the gate was opened by a servant.

'I hope you want nothing more, Pip. You'll get no more money from me,' Miss Havisham said when she saw me.

'That is not why I am here, Miss Havisham,' I replied. 'I want you to know I am doing well in my apprenticeship, that is all. I shall always be grateful to you.'

'Well, Pip, you can come and see me sometimes,' Miss Havisham answered. 'Come every year on your birthday. As you see, I am alone now.'

'I . . . I hope Estella is well,' I said.

'Estella is very well,' Miss Havisham replied. 'And she is more beautiful than ever. She is in France, being educated to be a lady.

'Do you feel that you have lost[5] her, Pip?' she added, with a cruel smile.

I could not answer. Miss Havisham laughed. I said goodbye to her and walked sadly home.

When I reached the forge, I was surprised to see a crowd of people outside.

I ran into the kitchen. Joe was there, and the doctor. My poor sister, Mrs Joe Gargery, was lying quiet and still on the floor.

Someone had attacked Mrs Joe when she was alone in the house. She was not dead, but terribly injured, unable to walk or speak.

My sister lay in bed for many weeks. At last she was able to sit downstairs. But her sharp voice was quiet for ever. She never spoke again. From that day onwards someone had to look after Mrs Joe all the time. And so Biddy came into our lives.

'I Must Become a Gentleman!'

Biddy was the same age as me. But she was not beautiful like Estella. How could she be beautiful? She was only a common girl from the village. But Biddy's eyes were bright. She had a sweet smile and was sensible and kind.

The years passed. I visited Satis House every year, on my birthday. I never saw Estella, but I did not forget her. I longed to be educated, like Estella. I wanted Estella to think well of me and to like me. I wanted Estella's respect and admiration. How stupid I was!

It was summer. One Sunday afternoon, Biddy and I went for a walk on the marshes. There were ships on the river, sailing slowly towards the sea. I remembered Estella, far away in another country. I began, as usual, to dream of my plans for the future.

We sat down by the river and watched the water flow slowly by.

'Biddy, I am going to tell you a secret,' I said. 'You must never speak of it to anyone.'

Biddy looked at me in surprise. She promised to tell no one.

'Biddy,' I went on, 'I hate being a blacksmith like Joe. I want to be a gentleman.'

Biddy smiled and shook her head.

'Oh no, Pip,' she answered. 'That wouldn't be right at all.'

'But I have important reasons for wanting to be a gentleman,' I told her.

'Don't you think you are happier as you are, Pip?' Biddy said gently.

'Happy?' I repeated. 'I can never be happy here, Biddy. Someone I admire and respect very much said I'm stupid and common. I must become a gentleman. I must.'

'Who called you stupid and common?' Biddy asked. 'That was not a true or a polite thing to say.'

'A young lady I met at Miss Havisham's,' I replied. 'The young lady is beautiful and I love her very much. She is the reason why I must become a gentleman.'

'Do you want to be a gentleman to hurt her or to make her respect you?' Biddy asked me quietly.

'I don't know.'

'I think you should forget her,' Biddy said. 'She has been rude and cruel to you. The young lady is not worth your respect.'

'You may be right, Biddy,' I said, 'I believe you are. But I love her very, very much.'

Tears came into my eyes. I threw myself on the ground in despair.

Biddy touched my hair gently.

'Thank you for telling me this, Pip,' she said. 'I will always keep your secret.'

I sat up.

'And I will always tell you everything, Biddy dear,' I said.

'Yes, I'm sure you will, Pip,' Biddy replied. She smiled sadly.

But I had not told Biddy everything. I believed that Miss Havisham had plans for me. I hoped that she would give me money for my education, money to make me a gentleman. If I had money and education, Estella would love me as I loved her. I hoped that Miss Havisham would make it possible for me to marry Estella.

6

Great Expectations

The months and years went by. I had been Joe's apprentice for four years.

One evening, Joe and I were sitting in the village inn. A stranger came in, a big, tall man, with heavy eyebrows. The man had large, very clean white hands. To my surprise, I recognized the man. I had seen him at Miss Havisham's, many years before. He had frightened me then. He frightened me a little now.

'I think there is a blacksmith here – name of Joe Gargery,' the man said in his loud voice.

'That's me!' Joe answered. He stood up.

'You have an apprentice, known as Pip,' the stranger went on. 'Where is he?'

'Here!' I cried, standing beside Joe.

'I wish to speak to you both. I wish to speak to you privately, not here,' the man said. 'Perhaps I could go home with you.'

We walked back to the forge in silence. When we were in the sitting room, the man began to speak.

'My name is Jaggers,' he said. 'I am a lawyer[2] in London, where I am well-known. I have some unusual business with young Pip here. I am speaking for someone else, you understand. A client[2] who doesn't want to be named. Is that clear?'

Joe and I nodded.

'I have come to take your apprentice to London,' the lawyer said to Joe. 'You won't stop him from coming I hope?'

'Stop him? Never!' Joe cried.

'Listen, then. I have this message for Pip. He has – great expectations!'

Joe and I looked at each other, too surprised to speak.

'Yes, great expectations,' Mr Jaggers repeated. 'Pip will one day be rich, very rich. Pip is to change his way of life at once. He will no longer be a blacksmith. He is to come with me to London. He is to be educated as a gentleman. He will be a man of property[2].'

And so, at last, my dream had come true. Miss Havisham – because Mr Jaggers' client *must* be Miss Havisham – had plans for me after all. I would be rich and Estella would love me!

Mr Jaggers was speaking again. 'There are two conditions,[2]' he said, looking at me. 'First, you will always be known as Pip. Secondly,' Mr Jaggers continued, 'the name of your benefactor[2]

'Listen,' said Mr Jaggers, 'I have this message for Pip.
He has – great expectations!'

is to be kept secret. One day, that person will speak to you, face to face. Until then, you must not ask any questions. You must never try to find out this person's name. Do you understand? Speak out!'

'Yes, I understand,' I answered. 'My benefactor's name is to remain a secret.'

'Good,' Mr Jaggers said. 'Now, Pip, you will come into your property when you come of age – when you are twenty-one. Until then, I am your guardian[2]. I have money to pay for your education and to allow you to live as a gentleman. You will have a private teacher. His name is Mr Matthew Pocket and you will stay at his house.'

I gave a cry of surprise. Some of Miss Havisham's relations were called Pocket. Mr Jaggers raised his eyebrows.

'Do you not want to live with Mr Pocket? Have you any objection to this arrangement?' he said severely.

'No, no, none at all,' I answered quickly.

'Good. Then I will arrange everything,' Mr Jaggers went on. 'Mr Pocket's son has rooms in London. I suggest you go there. Now, when can you come to London?'

I looked at Joe.

'At once, if Joe has no objection,' I said.

'No objection, Pip old chap,' Joe answered sadly.

'Then you will come in one week's time,' Mr Jaggers said, standing up. 'You will need new clothes. Here is some money to pay for them. Twenty guineas.'

He counted out the money and put it on the table.

'Well, Joe Gargery, you are saying nothing,' Mr Jaggers said to Joe sternly. 'I have money to give you too.'

'Money? What for?' Joe asked.

'For loss of your apprentice,' Mr Jaggers answered. 'Mr Pip has been your apprentice and now you are losing him.'

Dear Joe placed his heavy hand gently on my shoulder.

'Pip must go free,' Joe said 'Let him go free. Let him have

his good fortune[5]. No money can replace the dear child. We've always been the best of friends, Pip and me. Ever the best of friends . . . . [4]'

Joe could not say any more. He wiped away a tear.

And so my whole life changed. How happy I was! But Biddy and Joe were sad and quiet. This upset me. Why were they not pleased at my good fortune?

The next few days passed slowly for me. I bought new clothes, boots and a hat. I decided to say goodbye to Miss Havisham before I left for London.

'How smart you look, Pip!' Miss Havisham said when she saw me. 'You look like a gentleman. Why is this?'

'I have had good fortune since I last saw you, Miss Havisham,' I said with a smile. 'I am so grateful, Miss Havisham, so grateful.'

'I know, I know. I have seen Mr Jaggers, Pip,' Miss Havisham answered. 'He tells me you have great expectations. You now have a rich benefactor and you are leaving for London tomorrow.'

'Yes, Miss Havisham.'

'Well, be good then, Pip, and do what Mr Jaggers tells you. Goodbye, Pip. You must keep the name of Pip, you know.'

'Goodbye, Miss Havisham.'

Miss Havisham smiled and held out her hand. I bowed and kissed it.

On my last evening at the forge, Biddy cooked a special supper and I wore my new clothes.

The London coach left the town at six o'clock the next morning. I told Biddy and Joe that I wanted to walk to the town alone. Was I ashamed to be seen with them there? I'm afraid I was.

I said goodbye to Mrs Joe, then to Biddy and Joe. Biddy and Joe were both in tears as I waved goodbye for the last time.

I walked on and then my own tears began to fall. As I got nearer to the town, the morning mist disappeared and the sun shone. I was on my way to London. I was a young man with great expectations!

7

Learning to be a Gentleman

The journey took six hours and it was after midday when I reached London. I was amazed and frightened when I saw the city. London was crowded with hundreds of people and its streets were dirty.

I had the address of Mr Jaggers' office in Little Britain, Cheapside. After asking the way, I started to walk along the narrow crowded streets. At last, I found a door with "Mr Jaggers" written on it.

The open door led into a small office. A clerk was working there. He looked up as I walked in.

'Is Mr Jaggers here?' I asked nervously.

'Mr Jaggers is in court[2]. He won't be long,' the clerk answered. 'You are Mr Pip, I think. My name's Wemmick. Come and wait in Mr Jaggers' room.'

Mr Jaggers' room was a dark, gloomy place. Its small window was very dirty and no light came through it. There was a big black chair for Mr Jaggers and a smaller one, on which I sat.

Mr Wemmick, the clerk, went on with his work. Mr Jaggers' clerk was a short, neat man about fifty years old. He had a square face and a wide, thin mouth. His black eyes were very bright. On his fingers, he wore four or five silver and black rings.

By the time Mr Jaggers came back, several poorly dressed people were waiting for him. They all began talking at once. They wanted him to speak for them in court.

Mr Jaggers spoke to them all in a stern and angry way. When they had gone, he came in to see me.

Learning to be a Gentleman

'Here is your allowance[2], Pip,' he said. 'I think it's too much money but that's nothing to do with me. You'll get into debt[5], of course, all young men get into debt,' he added severely. 'You are going to live at Barnard's Inn with Mr Herbert Pocket. Wemmick will take you there.

'Wemmick!' Mr Jaggers then called out. 'Walk with Pip to young Mr Pocket's rooms.'

Wemmick gave me a wide smile. He led me through the busy streets, always looking straight in front of him.

'Here we are, Barnard's Inn,' Wemmick said, turning down a narrow street into a little square. He led me to the corner building and pointed up some steep stairs.

'Up there, top floor,' he added. 'As I look after your allowance I expect we shall meet often. Goodbye, Pip.'

I found Herbert's name on a door at the top of the stairs. Under his name, there was a piece of paper. It said, "Back soon".

I waited. A few minutes later, I heard quick footsteps on the stairs. A pale young man appeared, carrying a basket of strawberries.

'Mr Pip, isn't it?' the young man said, with a smile. 'I went to the market for some fruit. My father tells me you are to be my companion. I hope you will like living here. I'm sure we shall be friends.'

As the young man unlocked the door, I stared at him in surprise. Then he began to stare at me.

'Why, you are the boy I fought in Miss Havisham's garden!' Herbert exclaimed.

'And you are the pale young gentleman!' I answered.

We both laughed cheerfully and shook hands.

'It all seems so long ago,' Herbert said. 'Miss Havisham is my father's cousin. She's a very strange woman. You met Estella, of course. Miss Havisham adopted[5] her to take revenge.'

'Revenge? For what? What do you mean?' I asked.

'Don't you know?' Herbert replied. 'It's a very strange story. Mr Jaggers is your guardian, isn't he? He's Miss Havisham's lawyer too, and he knows all her secrets.'

'Why, you are the boy I fought in Miss Havisham's garden!'
Herbert exclaimed.

Learning to be a Gentleman

Whilst we ate dinner, Herbert told me all he knew.

'Miss Havisham's father died. She and her brother were very rich,' Herbert said. 'But the brother spent his money carelessly and was soon in debt.

'Miss Havisham's brother had a very wicked friend. He was dishonest and he was a liar. Miss Havisham fell in love with this man. My father tried to warn Miss Havisham, but she would not listen. The two young people decided to get married and all the arrangements were made for the wedding. But on the wedding day the bridegroom did not come. He sent Miss Havisham a letter saying he could not marry her.'

'And did Miss Havisham receive that letter at twenty minutes to nine, as she was dressing herself for the wedding?' I asked.

'Exactly at that time,' Herbert said. 'As you know, everything in the house stopped at that moment. Miss Havisham has not seen the daylight since.'

'When did she adopt Estella?' I asked.

'I don't know,' Herbert replied. 'As long as I have known Miss Havisham, Estella has been at Satis House.

'Miss Havisham wants to take revenge on all men,' he went on. 'Miss Havisham has brought up Estella to break men's hearts, because her own heart was broken.'

The next day, Herbert took me to his father's house in Hammersmith, to begin my education as a gentleman. I was to live there while I was studying. I also had my own room at Herbert's. We got on well together. Herbert taught me how to dress in smart London clothes. He also showed me how to behave like a gentleman. I was able to help Herbert pay for his rooms with my allowance.

Herbert had little money and no expectations. His rooms were almost empty and not very comfortable. I had the idea of buying carpets and some more furniture. But to get these things I needed more money. Feeling a little afraid, I went to Mr Jaggers.

'How much do you want?' said Mr Jaggers sharply.

'Well . . .' I began.

'Come, you must have an idea,' Mr Jaggers went on in his stern way. 'Shall we say fifty pounds?'

'Oh, not nearly so much as that,' I said quickly.

'Five pounds then?' Mr Jaggers suggested.

'Oh, more than that!' I exclaimed.

'More than five,' Mr Jaggers said slowly. 'How much more? Twice five? Three times? Four times five? Will that do?'

I told Mr Jaggers that twenty pounds would do very well.

'Wemmick!' Mr Jaggers cried, as he left the office. 'Give Mr Pip twenty pounds!'

'I don't think I understand Mr Jaggers,' I said to Wemmick when we were alone.

'He doesn't expect you to understand him. He doesn't want you to,' Wemmick replied. 'No one understands him – that's why he's so successful. Here's your money, Mr Pip.'

Another young man was studying with Mr Matthew Pocket. His name was Bentley Drummle. He came from a good family and he was very rich. Bentley Drummle was a gentleman but he did not behave like one. He was a big, awkward, clumsy young man. And he was proud and bad-tempered.

Mr Jaggers took an interest in Matthew Pocket's young gentlemen. One day he invited us all to his house for dinner.

The food was good and we had plenty to drink. Mr Jaggers liked to watch us talking and arguing. He was interested to see how much Drummle and I hated each other.

Dinner was served by Mr Jaggers' housekeeper. She was a tall woman of about forty. Her face was very pale, and her eyes were dark. Her long dark hair lay over her shoulders.

When the woman brought in the food, she looked only at Mr Jaggers. She was breathing quickly, as though she was afraid.

Learning to be a Gentleman

As he drank his wine, Bentley Drummle became more and more bad-tempered. He kept saying how strong he was. Very soon he and I had taken off our jackets to show how strong our arms were.

At that moment, the housekeeper came in to take the plates from the table. Mr Jaggers suddenly caught hold of one of her arms. He looked at us all and then spoke.

'If you want to see strength,' Mr Jaggers said, 'look at this woman's wrists. Molly, let them see your wrists – both of them.'

'Master, no,' the woman whispered, staring at Mr Jaggers with her strange, dark eyes.

'Show them, Molly,' Mr Jaggers said.

He held Molly's wrists down on the table.

'There's power in those wrists,' Mr Jaggers said. 'Few men have the strength this woman has. She has used it too. She was wild once, but I have broken her.

'That'll do, Molly,' Mr Jaggers said at last, letting go of his housekeeper's wrists. 'We have seen you. You can go.'

Mr Jaggers filled our wine glasses again. Very soon, Drummle and I were shouting at each other. We both stood up, ready to fight. But Mr Jaggers made us be quiet and told us it was time to go home.

I was ashamed of my behaviour. As we were leaving his house, I turned and apologized to Mr Jaggers.

'It's nothing, Pip,' Mr Jaggers replied. 'But be careful of that young man, Drummle. He's bad-tempered and cruel. He could be dangerous. Take care, Pip. Bentley Drummle will make a bad enemy.'

I followed Mr Jaggers' advice. I was pleased when Drummle completed his studies and left Mr Pocket's house.

I was so busy learning to be a gentleman, that I did not write to Joe and Biddy. They were part of my old life, a life I wanted to forget. I was a gentleman now. I did not want to remember that I had been a poor, uneducated blacksmith.

Then one day I received a letter.

'There's power in those wrists,' Mr Jaggers said. 'Few men have the strength this woman has.'

Learning to be a Gentleman

> *My dear Mr Pip,*
>
> *I am writing to you at the request of Mr Gargery. He is going to London and will call on you at nine o'clock on Tuesday morning. Your poor sister, Mrs Joe, is still not well. Mr Gargery and I talk about you every night.*
>
> *Your servant and friend,*
> *Biddy*

The letter arrived on Monday. I did not wish to see Joe, but I prepared a big breakfast for him. Herbert and I were ready and waiting long before nine o'clock.

At last I heard Joe's heavy step on the stairs. I heard him stop and slowly read my name on the door. Then he knocked.

'Joe, how are you, Joe?' I cried, as I opened the door.

'Pip old chap, how are you?' Joe answered, taking my hand in his.

Joe's honest face shone with joy. He shook my hand so much that I thought he would never stop.

Joe looked awkward and uncomfortable in his best clothes. He took off his hat and twisted it round and round in his great hands. He stared around the room and stared at my brightly coloured dressing gown[5].

'Well, what a gentleman you are, Pip!' he exclaimed.

'And you look well too, Joe,' I answered. 'Let me take your hat.' But Joe held his hat all through the meal.

'Tea or coffee, Mr Gargery?' Herbert asked politely.

'Thank you kindly, sir. I'll take whatever you'll be taking yourself,' Joe answered.

'Coffee then,' Herbert said cheerfully. But Joe looked so unhappy that, with a kind smile, Herbert gave him some tea.

Joe was uncomfortable and awkward with us and this made me angry. I was too stupid to see that it was my fault. I should not have been ashamed of him. I was glad when Herbert left us to go to work.

'Now we are alone, sir . . .' Joe began, but I interrupted him angrily.

'Why do you call me "sir", Joe?' I asked.

'Now we are alone, sir,' Joe repeated slowly, 'I must tell you why I am here, in the home of a gentleman.'

I said nothing.

'Well, sir – Pip,' Joe went on, 'Miss Havisham asked to see me. She has a message for you. And the message is that Estella has come home and would be glad to see you.'

At the sound of Estella's name, my heart began to beat very fast. I did not answer Joe. I could only think of Estella.

Joe stood up, twisting his hat in his hand.

'Don't leave, Joe,' I said. 'You must stay to dinner.'

'No, Pip old chap,' Joe answered. 'You are a gentleman now. It's not right for me to be here in London. But if you ever come back and visit us at the forge, you will be very welcome. Until then, I'll say goodbye. Goodbye and God bless you, Pip old chap.'

And before I could answer, Joe had gone.

I sat at the table, excited and confused. Miss Havisham had plans for Estella and me, that was clear. Miss Havisham had made me a gentleman, so that Estella could marry me. With joy in my heart, I began to prepare for my journey.

8

Young Men in Love

I left London early next morning. When I got to Satis House, I rang the bell as usual and a servant opened the gate. Taking a candle, I walked along the dark and gloomy corridors and up the stairs. I knocked on the door of Miss Havisham's dressing room.

'That's Pip's knock. Come in, Pip,' I heard Miss Havisham say.

When I opened the door, Miss Havisham was sitting by the dressing table as usual. Beside her, was an elegant[5] young woman who I had not seen before.

'Well, Pip?' Miss Havisham said.

'I heard that you wished to see me, Miss Havisham, so I came at once,' I said.

As I spoke, the elegant young lady looked up at me. It was Estella. She smiled.

'Has she changed, Pip?' Miss Havisham asked. 'She used to be proud and scornful. Do you remember?'

Although I was wearing my fine clothes, I felt clumsy and awkward. I was that common boy again who Estella had laughed at.

'Has Pip changed?' Miss Havisham asked Estella.

'Very much,' Estella answered.

As we talked, Estella's smile tore at my heart. The more I saw of her, the more I loved her.

'Isn't she elegant, isn't she beautiful? Don't you admire her, Pip?' Miss Havisham whispered.

'Everyone who sees Estella must admire her,' I replied.

'Then love her, love her, Pip!' Miss Havisham cried. 'It does not matter how she behaves towards you. If she is good to you, love her. If she tears your heart to pieces, love her, love her.

'Never forget, Pip,' Miss Havisham went on, 'you must give everything for real love. You must give your whole heart, as I did, as I did!'

And she fell back into her chair with a cry.

Before I left Satis House, Estella and I walked together in the garden. I reminded Estella how I had once fought Herbert there.

'Herbert and I are great friends now,' I said.

'Of course, with your new life, you have new friends,' Estella answered. 'The people who you knew before cannot be your companions now.'

I did not answer. Estella's words made me feel ashamed of Joe and Biddy. I decided not to visit them at the forge as I had planned.

We walked on and I showed Estella the place where I had cried. Estella stopped for a minute and looked at me.

'I have not changed, Pip,' she said. 'If we are to meet again, you must understand that. Remember, I have no love in my heart for anyone. No love in my heart at all.'

I heard Estella's words, but I did not believe them. Estella and I were going to be together. Miss Havisham had planned it.

But my love for Estella did not make me happy. I was in torment[5] when I saw her and in torment when I did not see her.

Back in London, I could no longer keep my feelings to myself. When Herbert and I were having dinner, I made a decision.

'My dear Herbert,' I began, 'I have something important to tell you. But it is a secret.'

Herbert smiled.

'Your secret will be safe with me, Pip,' he said.

I took a deep breath.

'Herbert! I must tell you. I love . . . I adore Estella!'

Herbert smiled again.

'I know that, my dear Pip,' Herbert said. 'I believe you adored her from the first moment you saw her!'

'You are right, Herbert,' I said. 'And now she is a beautiful and elegant young woman.'

'Then you are lucky that she has been chosen for you,' Herbert said cheerfully. 'But has Mr Jaggers ever said that Estella is part of your expectations, Pip?'

'No, never,' I said slowly.

'Then perhaps she is not part of your expectations. Perhaps you should not think of Estella so much,' Herbert said. 'Think of the way she has been brought up. Think of Miss Havisham. Estella has the power to make you very unhappy, Pip. Could you not forget her for a time?'

I shook my head.

'I have not changed, Pip,' Estella said. 'Remember I have no love in my heart for anyone.'

'No, that's impossible, quite impossible,' I replied.

'Well, then, I suppose there is nothing more to say,' Herbert said kindly.

'But you are not the only one in love, Pip,' Herbert added. 'I have a secret of my own. And my secret is – I am engaged to be married!'

'Congratulations, Herbert,' I said. 'May I know the lady's name?'

'Her name is Clara. She lives with her father, who is an invalid[5]. As I have no expectations and she is poor, we cannot marry yet. Not until I make my fortune!

'That means hard work,' Herbert went on. 'One day I shall have enough money to marry and then how happy Clara and I will be!'

How lucky Herbert was! He was poor, but Clara loved him. I was in love with a beautiful woman and I had great expectations. But Estella was proud and had no love in her heart for me.

Would Estella ever forget her pride and love me?

9

I Come of Age

I now come to a time of my life of which I am bitterly ashamed. I forgot my old friends, Joe and Biddy. I did not visit them at the forge. I spent too much money and got into debt. I thought only of the time when I would be twenty-one. The time when I would receive my fortune and be able to marry Estella.

One day, I received a message from Estella. It was a short note, but it made me very happy.

I Come of Age

> *Satis House*
>
> *I am coming to London in two days' time. Miss Havisham wants you to meet me at the coach office in Cheapside. The coach arrives at five o'clock.*
>
> *Yours,*
> *Estella*

I met Estella at the coach office and then took her to Richmond. She was more beautiful than ever. Estella was going to live in the house of an important lady. She was going to be introduced to the rich and powerful people of London society.

Now that Estella was living in London, I tried to see her as often as I could. I would often go to Richmond and wait for many hours outside her house, hoping to see her.

Sometimes Estella allowed me to see her and once she let me kiss her. But she was often as proud and cold as she had been in the old days.

At this time I started to get more and more into debt. Living in London cost a lot of money. I bought fashionable clothes and expensive food and drink. Herbert and I joined a club for young gentlemen, and we went to the theatre, the opera and well-known restaurants. But the allowance I received was not enough to pay all of my debts. And Herbert was poor and he did not have the expectation of a fortune. He could not pay his debts.

On my twenty-first birthday I would come of age. I would become a rich man of property. On that day I would receive my fortune. I waited anxiously for that day.

I had not seen Biddy and Joe for many months. Then one day, a letter arrived from Biddy with bad news. My sister, Mrs Joe, was dead.

I went by coach from London to the funeral in the country. My sister was buried near my parents, in that lonely churchyard near the marshes.

I Come of Age

As I stood in the graveyard beside Biddy and Joe, I thought of the convict I had met there long ago. In my mind, I saw his face and heard his terrible voice. I remembered how he had frightened me.

Now that Mrs Joe was dead, Biddy was going back to the village. She was going to teach in the school.

After supper, I walked with Biddy in the garden. Biddy told me, in her quiet way, how much Joe loved me and how good he was.

'I know that, Biddy,' I said quickly. 'I won't forget Joe now he's alone. I shall come here to see him often.'

Biddy said nothing.

'Didn't you hear what I said, Biddy?' I asked.

'Yes, Mr Pip.'

'Don't call me "Mr Pip", Biddy,' I said crossly. 'And why don't you answer my question?'

'Are you quite sure that you will want to come from London to see Joe?' Biddy said at last, looking at me carefully.

'What a terrible thing to say, Biddy!' I cried. 'You have shocked me very much.'

She did not answer.

I slept badly that night, for Biddy's words had upset me.

When I got up in the morning, Joe was already at work in the forge. I went in and shook him by the hand.

'Goodbye, dear Joe! I shall be back soon and often,' I said.

'Never too soon, sir, and never too often, Pip old chap,' Joe replied.

I shook hands with Biddy too, although I was still a little angry with her.

But Biddy was quite right, of course. In London, my thoughts were only of Estella and my great expectations. I did not go back to see Joe as I had promised.

And then, at last, it was my twenty-first birthday. Mr Jaggers

I Come of Age

called me to his office. I first shook hands with Wemmick and then went in to Mr Jaggers.

'Congratulations, Mr Pip,' the lawyer said. 'I expect you have some questions to ask me. I shall answer them if I can.'

I took a deep breath and began to speak.

'Am I going to learn the name of my benefactor today, Mr Jaggers?'

'No. Ask me another.'

'Will I know the name soon?'

'I can't answer that at the moment,' Mr Jaggers said. 'Have you another question?'

'Have I . . . anything to receive, sir?'

Mr Jaggers smiled and asked me a question.

'You are in debt, I suppose?'

I said nothing.

'Come, Pip, are you in debt or not?'

'I'm afraid I am, Mr Jaggers.'

'Of course. You know you are,' he said. 'Wemmick!' he called. 'Give Mr Pip that piece of paper. Now, take it in your hand and look at it, Pip.'

'This is a banknote for £500,' I said in surprise.

'Right. And that sum of money is yours, Pip. It is a small part of your expectations. You will have that sum of money each year. You will not get into debt. Later, you will learn the name of your benefactor. These are my instructions.'

I thought for a moment. 'Is it possible that my benefactor may come to London – or ask me to go anywhere else?'

'It is possible, but not yet,' Mr Jaggers said. 'That is all I have to say at present, Pip.'

As I left Mr Jaggers' office, I was already making plans. First of all, I must pay all my debts. Secondly, I wanted to help Herbert.

Herbert worked hard, but he had no money and no expectations. I knew that Herbert would not accept money from me. So, with Wemmick's help, I made arrangements for him to become a partner[5]

'Give Mr Pip that piece of paper,' Mr Jaggers said to Wemmick.
'Now, take it in your hand and look at it, Pip.'

I Come of Age

in a small business in London. He would work hard and soon be able to marry Clara. My expectations would help them both.

Soon after my birthday, I received a short note from Estella.

> *It is time for me to visit Miss Havisham. She tells me you must take me to Satis House. The day after tomorrow, if you please.*
>
> *Estella*

Everything at Satis House was the same. We sat together by the fire in the big room. Miss Havisham looked at Estella, proud of her beauty.

Estella told Miss Havisham about all her admirers. Miss Havisham asked many questions and listened to Estella's answers with a cruel smile.

As Estella was speaking, Miss Havisham held her arm tightly. But after a time, Estella moved away impatiently.

'Are you tired of me, you ungrateful girl?' Miss Havisham cried. 'Do you have a heart of stone?'

'I am what you have made me,' Estella answered, with a proud, hard look. 'You have looked after me. I owe you everything. What do you want from me now?'

'Love,' Miss Havisham answered sadly.

Estella laughed.

'You adopted me. You became my mother,' Estella said. 'All that I am, all that I have, is yours. But I cannot give you what you never gave me. Love.'

'I gave her love, didn't I?' Miss Havisham cried, looking at me. 'I gave her all the love I had – strong, burning love! You know I'm telling the truth.'

'Your love was not true love,' Estella answered coldly. 'Your plan has always been clear. You wanted revenge for the love you lost. I have learnt your lessons well. I have always followed your teaching.'

I Come of Age

'So proud, so hard,' Miss Havisham said, crying softly.

'Who taught me to be proud? Who praised me when I was hard?' Estella replied.

'But not proud and hard to me! You cannot be proud and hard to *me*, Estella!' Miss Havisham cried, holding out her arms to the beautiful girl.

Estella looked at Miss Havisham coldly.

'I have never forgotten the wrong done to you. I have behaved as you wanted me to behave,' Estella said. 'I am what you have made me. That is all.'

Miss Havisham sank down on the floor, crying bitterly. Her long white hair spread out around her.

'But I wanted you to love me! Love me!' she cried.

Estella, tall and straight, stared at the fire. After a time, we helped Miss Havisham to her feet. When I left, the two women were sitting side by side, silent in that terrible, decaying room.

In London, Estella had many admirers. Everywhere Estella went – to the theatre, to balls, to dinners – men fell in love with her. To my horror, Bentley Drummle was one of Estella's admirers. He was very rich and I thought that Estella made him believe that she liked him.

One night, at a ball, Drummle had been paying more attention to Estella than usual.

'Why do you let him near you, Estella?' I asked. 'Drummle is stupid and bad-tempered. All he has is money and his important family name. But you give him looks and smiles that you never give to me.'

Estella answered angrily.

'Do you want me to treat you like the others?' she asked. 'Do you want me to deceive and entrap[5] you?'

'Do you deceive and entrap Drummle then, Estella?'

'Yes. Him and many others. All of them but you, Pip. Will you never be warned?'

'About what?'
'Don't fall in love with me. It will bring you nothing but sorrow.'

10
Abel Magwitch

Two years passed and I was twenty-three years old. I was still living with Herbert, but we now had rooms near the river. Herbert's business was doing very well. His company now had offices overseas and Herbert often went away on business.

The weather had been stormy all day. The strong wind was blowing the rain hard against the windows. Herbert was in France on business, and I was alone.

A church bell struck eleven. I closed the book I was reading. It was time to go to bed. But as I stood up, I heard the sound of footsteps on the stairs.

For a moment, I felt afraid. Then I picked up the lamp and opened the door.

'Who's there? Who do you want?' I called.

'Mr Pip. Top floor,' a rough sounding voice answered.

'That is my name,' I said. 'Is anything wrong?'

'Nothing's wrong,' the voice replied.

I held the lamp higher.

A man was coming slowly up the stairs. He was about sixty years old. The man had long, grey hair that lay over his shoulders. His face was wrinkled and brown and he was roughly dressed.

To my surprise, the man was holding out his arms to greet me.

'Do you wish to come in? Have you business with me?' I asked.

'Yes, I wish to come in, master,' the man answered quietly. He walked slowly into the room. He looked around him with pleasure.

'What do you want?' I asked.

Abel Magwitch

The man took off his hat and sat down.

'Just give me a little time,' he said in his rough voice. 'I've come a long way and had a hard journey. You are alone here, aren't you?' he added.

'Why do you, a stranger, ask me that question?'

'A stranger?' the man repeated. 'That's a disappointing word to hear, when I've come so far. But you're a brave fellow, I can see that. Don't harm me, Pip. You'll be sorry if you do.'

And then I knew him. I fell back against the wall. He was the convict I had helped so long ago on the marshes!

The man stood up and again held out his arms to me.

'Yes, young sir. I am the convict you helped. You were brave then, my boy,' he said. 'I have never forgotten it, Pip, never.'

'Stop!' I cried, as he moved towards me. 'That was a long time ago. I was a little child then. I am pleased you are grateful. And I hope you have changed your way of life. But you must understand . . .'

The man looked at me sharply.

'Understand? What must I understand?' he said.

'. . . understand that our lives are different now,' I went on. 'There is no further reason for us to meet. But you are wet and you look tired. Let me get you a drink before you go.'

The man sat down again.

'I will have a drink before I go,' he said slowly. 'Hot rum and water, if you please.'

I prepared the drink quickly. When I handed him the glass, I saw that the old convict's eyes were full of tears.

I sat down near him with my own glass.

'I do not wish to be hard on you,' I said. 'Indeed, I wish you well. How have you been living?'

'I've been in Australia. I've been a sheep farmer, and I've done well, marvellously well,' the old convict replied.

'I am glad to hear it,' I said.

'Thank you, dear boy. And I see that you have done well since I last saw you. May I ask how?'

Abel Magwitch

'I . . . I've come into some property,' I said.

'May I ask what property? May I ask whose?'

For some reason, I began to shake with fear.

'I don't know,' I answered.

'Could I guess your yearly income, since you came of age?' the man asked quietly. 'Would it be - five hundred pounds?'

My heart was beating wildly now. I stood up and held tightly to the back of my chair. I stared at the man in terror.

'I suppose you had a guardian. A lawyer maybe?' the convict went on. 'Did his name begin with J?'

I could not speak. I felt faint and the room began to move around me.

'Do you want to know how I found you?' the convict went on. 'Well, that lawyer has a clerk called Wemmick. He sent me your address.'

I could not breathe. I gave a cry and almost fell to the ground. The old convict caught hold of me and placed me gently on a chair.

'Yes, Pip, dear boy,' he said. 'It's me what's made[4] a gentleman of you. I swore that I would make you a gentleman and I have. Every guinea I've made has been for you. I've lived a poor life, so that you could live well. Yes, Pip, that starving convict you met on the marshes has made you a gentleman. I've sent money all these years for you to spend. And now I've come to see the gentleman I've made!

'Look at your clothes,' he went on, 'a gentleman's clothes. And these are your books,' he added, looking around the room. 'Hundreds and hundreds of books. You shall read them to me, dear boy, for I've had no education. But it's me what's had you educated. I'm proud of you, Pip, dear boy, proud!'

And he took my cold hands and put them to his lips.

I felt very ill. I could not speak.

'Don't try to talk, Pip,' the old convict went on. 'You weren't prepared for this, I see. Didn't you ever think it could be me?'

'Never, no, never!' I whispered.

Abel Magwitch

'Well, it was me. And no one knew about it but Mr Jaggers.'

The old man smiled. 'How good looking you've grown, my boy,' he said. 'You're in love with a beautiful girl, I'm sure. She shall be yours, if money can help you.'

Estella, oh, Estella, I thought.

'Yes, you've grown to be a fine gentleman, Pip,' the convict said. 'I promised myself I would see you one day, and now I have. It wasn't safe to come, but I came.'

'Not safe? What do you mean?' I asked in surprise.

'I was transported for life[2],' he answered quietly. 'If you're sent as a convict to Australia, it's death to return. If I am caught, I shall be hanged, hanged by the neck until I'm dead.'

I held my head in my hands. This wretched man was my benefactor! By coming to see me, he had ruined all my dreams. And he had put his own life in danger too.

I could not send him away. I stood up slowly. I closed the shutters over the windows and locked the door. I prepared the bed in Herbert's room for the man and, at last, he went to sleep.

Later, I sat by the fire, trying to think. Miss Havisham's plans for me? All a dream. Estella? She was not meant for me.

And because of this man, a convict, I had forgotten Joe and Biddy. I could never undo the wrong I had done them.

What should I do with the man in the next room? What was going to become of him? What was going to become of me?

At last I fell asleep by the fire. I awoke to hear the church bell striking five. The room was dark. The wind was still blowing the rain hard against the windows.

I made breakfast. The old convict ate in great mouthfuls. I was disgusted by him. He then lit his pipe and stood in front of the fire. He took out a wallet of money and threw it onto the table.

'There, my boy, spend that,' he said. 'I've come back to see my boy spend money like a gentleman!'

Abel Magwitch

'No, no, we must talk!' I cried. 'I don't even know your name. How long are you staying in England? Where do you plan to live?'

'My name is Magwitch, Abel Magwitch,' he said. 'And I'm staying in England for ever, though it's death by hanging if I'm caught.'

I decided that I had to speak to Mr Jaggers. Leaving Magwitch alone, I locked the door of my rooms and hurried to the lawyer's office.

When he saw me, Mr Jaggers held up his hand.

'Don't tell me anything – I don't want to know,' he said quickly.

'I must know one thing, Mr Jaggers,' I said. 'I have been told something about my benefactor. Is it true?'

'You cannot have been "told" anything. "Told" means you have talked to that person. You cannot have talked to him. He is in Australia. You must have been "informed",' Mr Jaggers warned me.

I understood then that Mr Jaggers knew Abel Magwitch was in England. And he knew that his client was in danger.

' "Informed", then,' I agreed, ' "informed" that Abel Magwitch is my benefactor.'

'That is true. Your benefactor is the man in Australia.'

'But I thought that Miss Havisham . . .' I began.

'You have misunderstood. Miss Havisham was never your benefactor. Your benefactor is far away. But he has plenty of money for you. You will have it soon.'

I did not want the money now. I knew that Estella would never be mine. I left Mr Jaggers' office without another word.

On my way home I bought some new clothes for Abel Magwitch. But when I had cut his hair and he was dressed in the new clothes, he still looked like a convict – a murderer perhaps. The more I saw the man, the more I feared and hated him.

Herbert returned from France that afternoon. When I heard his step on the stairs, I opened the door quickly.

'Hello, Pip!' Herbert said cheerfully. Then he added, 'How pale you look! What's the matter?'

Abel Magwitch

Then he saw Magwitch.

'Who is this?' he asked in surprise.

'Herbert, my dear friend,' I said, shutting and locking the door behind him, 'something very strange has happened.'

Before I could explain, Magwitch took a little black bible from his pocket and held it out to Herbert.

'Take the Holy Book in your right hand, dear boy,' he said to him. 'Swear to God that you will never repeat what Pip is going to tell you.'

'Do it, Herbert,' I whispered. So Herbert took the bible and repeated the words and then the old convict shook him by the hand.

'Now you have sworn on the Bible. God has heard your promise. Sit down and listen to what Pip is going to tell you.'

So I told Herbert everything.

'I need your help, Herbert,' I said at last. 'What should I do now?'

'My poor dear Pip,' Herbert exclaimed. 'I am so confused that I cannot think clearly. But the first thing is to find rooms for . . . Mr Magwitch. Then, I'm afraid, there is only one thing to do.'

Herbert turned to Abel Magwitch, who was listening carefully.

'You must leave England,' Herbert told him. 'Go to France or Germany. You will be safe there. And you must go with him, Pip,' Herbert went on. 'This man's life is in danger because he came to see you. It is only right that you should get him out of danger.'

I stared at the floor unhappily. I did not care where I went. I had no expectations now – for I could never take money from Magwitch again. My life had been ruined by this man who I hated and feared.

'Very well,' I said at last. I turned to Magwitch.

'If I am to help you, I must know everything about you. Why were you put in prison? Who was that other man on the marshes? Tell us.'

He stared at the fire for a moment and then began to speak.

'Dear boy and Pip's friend, my story can be told in a very few words,' the convict began. 'I don't know where I was born. I know

Before I could explain, Magwitch took a little black bible from his pocket and held it out to Herbert.

nothing about myself but my name. The first thing I remember was stealing food to keep alive. In jail and out of jail, in jail and out. I was punished wherever I went. I had no education. I only learnt to read and write a little.'

Magwitch stopped for a moment and then went on.

'About twenty years ago, I met Compeyson, the man I fought on the marshes. He looked like a gentleman, but he was very wicked and very clever. He asked me to help him with his plans. And he made sure, that if anything went wrong, I would be blamed for it.

'Compeyson had a friend, a young man with a rich sister. The two men treated this woman very badly and stole her money.'

When Herbert heard this, he looked up quickly, but he said nothing.

'Later, the young man died,' Magwitch went on. 'Compeyson had more and more power over me. All the wicked things he planned were done by me. When we were caught, I was blamed for everything. I sold everything I had to pay the lawyer, Mr Jaggers, to speak for me in court. But when Compeyson and me stood up in court, he was dressed like an honest gentleman and I looked wicked and dishonest. So he was sent to prison for seven years. I was sent to prison for fourteen years. And we were both sent to the Hulks.

'One day, I had a fight with Compeyson and cut his face. I escaped from the Hulks onto the marshes. That's where you helped me, dear boy. When I found out that Compeyson had escaped too, I caught him and waited for the soldiers to come. So instead of escaping, I was transported to Australia for life.'

'And Compeyson?' I asked quietly. 'Where is he now?'

'I never heard of him again. He may be alive or dead. I don't know. But if he finds me here, it's death for me or him!'

The old convict said no more, but smoked his pipe and stared at the fire.

Herbert passed a piece of paper to me. On it, he had written these words:

> *Miss Havisham's brother was the young man. Compeyson was the man who was going to marry her. But he stole her money and left her on her wedding day.*

I looked at Herbert, but said nothing. I was trying to think.

If Compeyson was alive, he might find out that Magwitch had returned. Herbert was right. Magwitch was in danger in London. I had to take the old man away as soon as possible.

That same day, we found a cheap room for him to stay in. Some days later, Herbert took Magwitch to the house where Clara lived with her father. The house was at Old Mill Bank, a quiet place, near the river. Magwitch could live there on the top floor. As soon as possible, we would get him out of England.

We told Wemmick of our plan. He promised to warn us if anyone asked about Magwitch.

Every time I went out, I thought that someone was following me. Was Compeyson alive and in London? Had he seen his old enemy? Did Compeyson know about me and Abel Magwitch?

11

Secrets from the Past

My expectations were at an end. Miss Havisham was not my benefactor. Estella could not be mine. But I had to see her again.

I found out that Estella was staying with Miss Havisham, and I decided to go to Satis House for the last time.

Once more I walked through the dark, dusty corridors of Satis

House. I found Miss Havisham and Estella sitting together in the dressing room. Estella was knitting[5]. Both women looked at me in surprise.

'Why are you here, Pip?' Miss Havisham asked.

'I have something that I must say to you, Miss Havisham,' I replied. 'I have found out who my benefactor is, and I am very unhappy. I thought it was you. You knew that I thought this. But you did not tell me my mistake. Was that kind, Miss Havisham?'

'Kind? Do you expect me to be kind, Pip?' Miss Havisham answered, hitting her stick on the floor angrily.

'I expect nothing from you, Miss Havisham,' I said quietly. 'I have come because I need your help, but not for myself.'

'Who do you want me to help?' Miss Havisham asked. 'What do you want, Pip?'

'Two years ago, I was able to help my good friend, Herbert Pocket. I paid money for him to become a partner in a business,' I explained. 'He does not know who did this. Now I need more money, to complete my plans for him. I cannot take money from my benefactor. Can you help me?'

At first Miss Havisham said nothing. Then she spoke.

'Have you anything else to say, Pip?' she asked.

I looked at Estella. She went on knitting and did not raise her head.

'Estella,' I said, 'you know I love you. I have always thought that Miss Havisham wanted us to marry. I know now that this is not true. But I must tell you that I love you and always will.'

'Love is a word I do not understand,' Estella answered. 'I tried to warn you, Pip, but you didn't listen. I am going to be married, but not to you.'

'Then who . . .?' I began.

'Bentley Drummle,' Estella said quietly.

'Estella! That can't be true!' I cried. 'He is stupid and cruel. You will never be happy with him.'

'Do you think he will be happy with me?' Estella said, with a cold smile. 'I know nothing of happiness or love. You will soon forget me, Pip.'

'You are part of my life, part of every breath I take,' I whispered. 'I shall never forget you, Estella, never. God bless you and forgive you.'

I kissed her hand. I do not remember leaving the room.

I was in despair. Without waiting for the coach, I set off to walk the long road to London.

It was after midnight when I reached home. I climbed the stairs to our rooms, desperate and exhausted. Fixed to the door was a piece of paper.

> Don't stay here tonight. Go to Old Mill Bank at eight tomorrow night. Burn this note.

The message was in Wemmick's writing.

I stayed at an inn and waited for the hours to pass. At eight o'clock that night, I was outside the house at Old Mill Bank. I knocked at the door and Herbert opened it.

He took me inside and spoke quietly.

'He is safe now,' Herbert said, 'but there is danger. Wemmick found out and warned us. Come upstairs and see Magwitch.'

Abel Magwitch was sitting quietly by the window of his room. He was looking at the river below him. His face looked old and gentle now.

'I'm pleased to see you, dear boy,' he said. 'Compeyson is in London, looking for me. Compeyson found out that I had come to see you. But Herbert thinks I am safe here and Jaggers knows everything.'

'This is a good place to be, for another reason,' Herbert told me. 'When you and Magwitch are ready to leave, we can row[5] him down the river ourselves. You can get on board a ship at the mouth of the river[5]. Compeyson will not expect you to escape like this. You will soon be far away.'

Secrets from the Past

'When do we go?' I asked quickly.

'Soon, Pip,' Herbert said. 'First, we'll buy a boat and row up and down the river every day. People will get used to seeing us. They will think we enjoy rowing on the river. Meanwhile, I will come here as usual. When I visit Clara, I can see Magwitch. You must not come here, Pip. Compeyson wants you to lead him to Magwitch.'

We followed Herbert's plan. Herbert and I rowed on the river nearly every day.

No stranger went near Old Mill Bank, but I was unhappy. I spent many hours walking the streets alone.

One evening, I met Mr Jaggers. 'Come and dine with me, Pip,' the lawyer said. 'I have something for you.'

When we were sitting in Mr Jaggers' house, he gave me a note from Miss Havisham. She wanted to see me on business. I decided to go to Satis House the next day.

'Well, Pip,' Mr Jaggers said, as we sat down to eat, 'I hear that Estella is married. She is Mrs Bentley Drummle now. There will be only one master in that marriage – Mrs Bentley Drummle!'

As Mr Jaggers was speaking, Molly, his housekeeper, placed our food on the table. As she stood behind her master, Molly moved her hands nervously. She moved her hands as though she was knitting.

I looked at the woman's dark eyes, her long, dark hair and her moving fingers. Where had I seen hair and movements like that before?

I remembered the last time I had seen Estella and a strange idea came into my mind. I grew pale and my heart began to beat very fast.

I did not speak, but Mr Jaggers saw me looking at Molly. When Molly left the room he slowly nodded his head. I had not asked the question, but he had answered it.

It was true! Molly was Estella's mother! And only Mr Jaggers and I knew the truth.

The next day, I went to Satis House. Miss Havisham was in the big room with the long table. She was sitting in a chair by the fire.

She agreed to help Herbert. When we had finished our business, she looked at me sadly.

'Are you very unhappy, Pip?' she asked.

'Yes, Miss Havisham. I am. There are many things making me unhappy. You know about one of them.'

Suddenly, Miss Havisham fell down on her knees.

'Oh, what have I done? What have I done?' she cried. 'Estella is married. Do you know that?'

'Yes.'

'Then forgive me, Pip. Forgive me for making you unhappy.'

'I forgive you, Miss Havisham,' I answered. 'I am to blame for my unhappiness too. But Estella is also unhappy. You should ask her for forgiveness. You have made her what she is.'

'Yes, yes, I know it!' Miss Havisham cried. 'I adopted her when she was a little child. I was unhappy and wanted revenge. I took away love from her heart and put ice in its place. If you knew my story, you would understand!'

'Miss Havisham, I do know your story,' I answered. 'I know why you adopted Estella and taught her to be cruel. I do not hate you, Miss Havisham. I am sorry for you.'

I helped Miss Havisham back into her chair by the fire. Then I left the room quietly.

I went downstairs and walked up and down in the garden. A feeling of great sadness filled my heart as I stood in that unhappy place.

I knew I would never return to Satis House. I ran upstairs quickly to see Miss Havisham for the last time. She was sitting quietly by the fire and did not move.

As I turned to go, a great flame sprang up suddenly from the fire. The flame leapt onto Miss Havisham's old, torn clothes. As I stood there, she ran towards me crying out in terror. Her torn clothes were burning fiercely.

I pulled off my heavy coat and threw it over the screaming woman, pushing her down. Then I dragged the cloth from the table

As I turned to go, a great flame sprang up suddenly from the fire.
The flame leapt onto Miss Havisham's old, torn clothes.

to cover her. The remains of the ruined wedding feast crashed down. There were clouds of dust, and mice and spiders ran across the floor. Miss Havisham screamed and screamed with pain.

Hearing Miss Havisham's cries, the servants rushed in. We laid Miss Havisham on the table and covered her gently. She was badly burned and could not be moved. Over and over again, she repeated the same words.

'What have I done? What have I done? Forgive me, oh, forgive me!'

A servant went to fetch a doctor. But he could not help her.

Miss Havisham lay there for several hours. I stayed with her, until, calm at last, she died.

My hands and arms had been badly burnt. Herbert came to Satis House and he took me back to London. There he looked after me. He was kind and gentle.

At first, my mind was confused, but, with Herbert's help, I slowly grew stronger.

My first thoughts were for Magwitch.

'He is safe,' Herbert told me. 'But as soon as you are well, we must help him to escape.

'I like him better now,' Herbert went on. 'We have talked together many times. Did you know he once had a wife, Pip? Magwitch's wife was a wild young woman and very jealous. She thought another woman wanted to steal her husband. So she fought the woman and the woman died. Magwitch's wife was put on trial for murder.'

'Murder?' I repeated in horror.

'Yes, murder. She was put on trial, but Mr Jaggers was her lawyer. He spoke for her in court and she was acquitted[2].

'Magwitch and this woman had a child, a little girl,' Herbert went on. 'Magwitch loved the child very much. But after the trial, the woman and the child disappeared. Magwitch never saw them again.'

'Herbert,' I said slowly, 'how long ago did these things happen?'

Secrets from the Past

'About twenty years ago,' Herbert answered. 'Three or four years before Magwitch saw you in the churchyard. You reminded him of the child he had lost.'

I sat up slowly.

'Herbert,' I said, 'I have something to tell you. I am sure it is the truth. The man we are hiding, Abel Magwitch, the returned convict, is Estella's father.'

As soon as I was strong enough, I went to see Mr Jaggers. 'We know who Estella's mother is, Mr Jaggers,' I told him.

'Estella's mother, Pip?' Mr Jaggers said carefully.

'Yes. I have seen her in your house, Mr Jaggers.'

The lawyer said nothing.

'I now know something more – the name of Estella's father,' I went on.

Mr Jaggers looked at me sharply.

'His name is Abel Magwitch,' I said, 'and Abel Magwitch is the man who is my benefactor.'

'Why does Magwitch think this?' Mr Jaggers asked in surprise.

'He doesn't think this,' I answered. 'He does not know that his daughter is alive.'

I told Mr Jaggers everything I knew and the things I had guessed. 'Mr Jaggers,' I said at last, 'terrible things have happened to all these people. They must be told the truth.'

Mr Jaggers thought for a time before he spoke.

'Perhaps you are right in what you have guessed, Pip. But who would be helped by knowing the truth now? Would the mother be helped? Or the father? Or the child?

'Think carefully, Pip. No one would be helped by knowing the truth, no one.'

Mr Jaggers was right. I thought of Estella. She had married a rich man from a proud family. But she was the daughter of a convict. The truth would destroy her. She must never know it.

12
Escape

It was now March. My burnt hands and arms had healed. Herbert and I decided it was time for Magwitch to leave England. I liked the old convict very much now, though I refused to accept his money. I had to help him. I had to get him to a safe place.

We found that a ship was leaving London for Hamburg in a few days' time. The big paddle steamer[5] would come down the Thames at high tide[5]. Our plan was to row down the river towards the sea. Magwitch would be dressed as a river pilot. He would carry a black bag and wear a thick cloak. The captain of the steamer needed a river pilot to guide him along the river to the sea. Magwitch and I would board the steamer and leave England for ever.

The day came for us to leave. In the evening, Herbert and I left our rooms and rowed down the river to Old Mill Bank. Magwitch was waiting for us.

He got into the boat and sat down.

'Dear boy, faithful dear boy. Thank you, thank you,' he said quietly.

His voice was more gentle now. He was peaceful and quiet. For the first time in his life, people had cared for him and spoken to him kindly. And so he was no longer the wild and terrible man I had first met.

'If all goes well, you will be a free man in a few hours,' I told him.

'Well, I hope so, dear boy. The water is moving quietly and there seems to be no danger,' he said. 'But we don't know what will happen, today or in the future.'

We rowed all night. Sometimes Herbert rowed. Sometimes I rowed. We stopped from time to time, to rest and eat. We listened for the sound of another boat, but we heard nothing. No one was following us.

Escape

By the time it was light, we were a long way down the river. We moored by the bank and waited for the great paddle steamer to pass.

When we saw the smoke of the steamer, we started rowing again. We rowed strongly towards the middle of the river.

Then, to my horror, I saw another boat moored ahead of us. When we had passed, it moved quietly out from the bank to follow us. It was a larger and faster boat than ours. Two men were rowing together.

There were four men in the boat. Three of the men were wearing uniforms. They were Customs[2] men. The fourth man sat in the back of the boat with his face covered.

The big steamer was nearer now. The shadow of the huge ship fell upon our small rowing boat. The steamer came nearer and nearer and its great paddles turned in the water with a terrible noise.

Suddenly, the Customs boat leapt ahead of us.

'You have a convict from Australia there!' a man shouted. 'His name is Abel Magwitch. I am here to arrest that man. Stop and give him to us!'

The great steamer came nearer and nearer. The people on board shouted when they saw the two boats far below.

'Stop the paddles! Stop the paddles!' they cried.

The two rowing boats were touching each other now. Suddenly, Magwitch leant across and pulled the cloak from the fourth man's face. On the man's face was a long scar.

'Compeyson! I knew it was you!' Magwitch cried. As he grabbed the man, there was another shout from the steamer. The boats turned round and round in the rough water. The paddles of the steamer were now above our heads.

Our boat overturned. The water roared in my ears. I was turned over and over by the crashing water from those terrible paddles.

A moment later, I was pulled roughly into the other boat. Herbert was there too. But our boat had gone. And where were Magwitch and Compeyson?

The paddle steamer had moved on now and the Customs men

Magwitch leant across and pulled the cloak from the fourth man's face. On the man's face was a long scar.

were looking down into the water. Then I saw Magwitch. He was swimming, but his heavy clothes were pulling him under the water. The Customs men grabbed him and pulled him into the Customs boat. Chains were put on his wrists and ankles.

Magwitch had been badly injured by the turning paddles.

'I think Compeyson's gone to the bottom of the river, dear boy,' he whispered to me. 'I had him in my arms. Then he fought free and the paddles hit him.'

The Customs men soon stopped looking for Compeyson. As we were rowed back to London in the Customs boat, I held the old convict's hand in mine. This rough, hard man had remembered my kindness to him long ago. He had treated me better than I had treated Joe!

'Dear boy,' Magwitch whispered, 'use my money when I've gone. One thing I ask – come to the court and see me for the last time. They will hang me now.'

'I will stay with you until the end,' I said. 'I will be as faithful to you as you have been to me.'

There was no hope for a returned convict. Magwitch was tried and sentenced to death by hanging. But he was very ill. His injuries were very bad. He was taken from the court to the prison hospital. I sat with him every day.

Every day, Magwitch grew weaker. One day, when I visited him, I felt that his death was near. He was pale and very weak.

'Dear boy, God bless you,' he whispered, as I sat down by the bed. 'You never left me even when there was danger. You stayed near me when the dark clouds gathered. This has been the best part of my life.'

His breathing was very bad now. He lay back on the bed and closed his eyes. I held his hand in mine.

'Dear Magwitch, I have something to tell you,' I said quietly. 'Can you understand what I say?'

The old convict held my hand tightly.

'You had a child once, who you loved and lost,' I said slowly. 'She lived and found rich friends. She is a lady now and very beautiful. And I love her.'

With the last of his strength, Abel Magwitch raised my hand to his lips. He opened his eyes and looked at me. Then he smiled and his eyes closed again – for ever.

13

Friends Together

And now followed the most terrible time of my life. Magwitch had wanted me to have his money, but when he was sentenced to death, the court took his money and property. I had many debts and no money to pay them. When Magwitch died, Herbert was abroad on business. I was alone.

I became very ill – I had a fever and could neither move nor speak. In my feverish dreams I remembered everything that had happened to me. My thoughts were strange and confused.

I thought I was in the river again, turning over and over in the crashing water. Then I thought I was a little child, sitting beside Joe. More and more in my dreams, the face I saw was Joe's. Joe, who had always been kind, had always been ready to help me. Joe, to whom I had been so unkind and so ungrateful.

Then one day, I opened my eyes. I was very weak, but the fever had gone. And there was Joe, sitting quietly by the window, smoking his pipe and smiling at me.

'Is that really you, Joe?' I said.

'Of course it is, Pip old chap. Waiting to help you as always, Pip.'

'Oh, Joe, I've been so ungrateful,' I said. 'Why are you so good to me?'

'You and me were ever the best of friends, Pip,' Joe answered.

'When you're well enough, we'll leave London and go back to the country, Pip old chap!'

'How long have I been ill, Joe?' I asked.

'How long?' Joe repeated slowly. 'Well, it's the end of May now. Tomorrow is the first of June.'

'And have you been here all this time, Joe?'

'That's right, old chap. Mr Jaggers told us you were ill. Biddy said I must come to you at once, so I did. Biddy is a very good woman. She loves you Pip and so do I. Biddy has taught me to read and write. She has told me to write to her about you.'

As I grew stronger, I told Joe everything. I told him how rich I had been and that now I was poor. But Joe did not want to hear.

'Pip old chap, we've always been the best of friends,' Joe said. 'Why try to explain what's past?

'When you was a child, I tried to save you from Mrs Joe and Tickler. Now I want to keep these troubles from you. There's no need for money to come between us. It never did before.'

With Joe's help, I was soon able to walk a little. My fever had completely gone and I felt better every day.

But one thing worried me. As I grew stronger, Joe became more awkward and uncomfortable with me. He even began to call me "sir".

One night, Joe came into my room and asked me how I was.

'Dear Joe, I am completely well now, thanks to you,' I answered.

Joe touched my shoulder with his great hand.

'Then goodnight, sir,' he whispered.

In the morning, I got up and dressed. I called to Joe, but he was not in his room. His luggage had gone.

Joe had left a note on the table.

As you are well again, I am leaving you. You will do better without Joe now.

Ever the best of friends,
Joe

With the note, were all my bills. Joe had paid all my debts.

I knew what I had to do. I would go back to the forge and ask Joe to let me live there. I would live and work there for a short time. Then I would go overseas and work for Herbert.

Later on, I would marry Biddy and live with her as a poor man. It was best to forget Estella. My great expectations were at an end. I would be a happier man without them.

It was late June and the weather was very beautiful. I walked slowly along the road to our village. I was enjoying the quiet peace of the fields and paths that I knew so well.

In the country I could live a simple life with Biddy. Joe would be nearby at the forge. Here I would forget the past and all my foolish dreams.

The village school, where I thought I would find Biddy, was closed. I walked on to the forge, and that too was closed.

But all the windows of our house were open wide. There were clean curtains at the windows and the little garden was bright with flowers.

And there, in the doorway, stood Joe and Biddy, holding hands. When they saw me, they laughed with pleasure.

'My dear Biddy, how smart you look!' I said. 'And you too, Joe,' I added. 'What's the matter?'

'It's my wedding day, Pip!' Biddy cried. 'And I'm married to Joe!'

So my last dream disappeared.

'Dear Biddy, you have the best husband in the world,' I said. 'And you, dear Joe, have the best wife. She will make you very happy, my dear, dear, Joe.

'I have come to thank you for everything you have done for me,' I said. 'One day, I shall have enough money to pay you back, Joe.

'Perhaps you will have a child, a little boy,' I went on. 'Tell him how I love and respect you both. Teach him to grow up a better man than me. And forgive me, dear Joe, for the wrong I have done you.'

'Pip, dear old chap, there is nothing to forgive,' Joe said. 'God knows, there is nothing to forgive.'

'Nothing to forgive, Pip dear, nothing to forgive,' Biddy whispered.

A month later, I left England and went to Egypt. I worked there as a clerk for Herbert. He and his partner were doing well, and, after a few years, I became a partner too. Herbert married Clara and I paid back my debt to Joe.

I worked in Egypt for eleven long years. I did not return to England in all that time.

Then, one evening in December, I returned to the old forge. I opened the kitchen door quietly and looked in. There was Joe, sitting in his place by the fire, And there, sitting on a stool next to him, was a little boy.

'We called him Pip, after you,' Joe said. 'We hoped he would grow like you, and we think he has!'

'I am very pleased, Joe,' I said.

'I do not think that I shall ever marry and have children,' I went on. 'But I shall love young Pip as if he were my own son.'

'But you *will* marry and have children of your own, Pip,' Biddy told me, with a smile.

'That's what Herbert and Clara say,' I replied. 'But I shall never marry.'

'Dear Pip,' Biddy said softly, 'Are you sure you still don't long for Estella? I'm sure you have not forgotten her.'

'My dear Biddy, I have forgotten nothing of my past life,' I answered. 'But that dream has gone, like all the others.'

I knew that Estella's marriage had been unhappy. Her husband,

Friends Together

Bentley Drummle, had died, but I was sure that Estella had married again.

After supper, I decided to visit the place where Estella and I had first met. I walked slowly from the forge and it was almost dark when I reached the tall iron gates. Satis House had been pulled down and the old garden was completely overgrown. Only the gates and the garden wall were standing. I walked in the garden in the evening mist. The moon and a few stars shone in the sky.

A woman was walking in the garden. As I got closer to her she turned and spoke my name.

'Estella,' I answered quietly.

'I am surprised that you recognize me,' Estella replied. 'My sad life has changed me, Pip.'

Estella was still beautiful. But there was a sadder, kinder look in her eyes. She touched my hand gently.

'It is strange that we should meet here, Estella, after so many years,' I said. 'Do you often come back?'

'I have never returned until today. All this belongs to me now. It is all I have left. You have been working overseas, I think.'

'Yes,' I answered. 'I work hard and I am doing well.'

'I have often thought of you, Pip,' Estella said.

'You have always been in my thoughts,' I answered.

'It is strange to be here, in the old place again,' Estella said. 'I have changed. I am a better person, I hope. You were kind to me all those years ago, Pip. Be kind to me now. Let us part from each other as friends.'

'We are friends,' I answered, 'friends who will never part. For now I have met you again, Estella, I will never let you go.'

Estella smiled. I held her hand and we walked together out of the overgrown garden. And I knew that, this time, we would never, never part.

A woman was walking in the garden. As I got closer to her she turned and spoke my name.

Points for Understanding

1

1 The person telling this story calls himself Pip. What is his real name?
2 At the start of the story, Pip is in a graveyard.
   (a) What is he doing there?
   (b) Who does he meet?
   (c) What does this person ask Pip to do?
3 Who does Pip live with? Describe these people.
4 Pip returns late to the forge. He is frightened of many things. Who and what is he frightened of?
5 What does Pip learn about the great guns and the Hulks?
6 Pip steals food and a file. Where does he take these things and who does he meet?

2

1 Why is Pip scrubbed clean and wearing his best clothes at half past one on Christmas Day?
2 What do you know about Uncle Pumblechook?
3 'What's happened to the meat pie?' Pip's sister asks. Describe what happens next.
4 Joe has to do some work that afternoon. What work is it?
5 What happens on the marshes?

3

1 What does Pip try to teach Joe?
2 Mrs Joe and Uncle Pumblechook bring some news from town. What is this news?
3 What happens when Pip and Uncle Pumblechook reach the gate of Satis House?
4 Who does Pip meet inside the house? What is strange about this person?
5 'He's just a common, working boy. What heavy boots he's wearing!'
   (a) Who says these things?
   (b) Who is she talking about?
6 What does Pip think about the people in Satis House?
7 How do you think Pip feels when he leaves Satis House?

4

1. What does Pip tell Mrs Joe about his visit to Satis House? Why do you think he says these things?
2. On his second visit to Satis House, Pip meets a stranger. Describe this man.
3. Pip goes into a different room with Miss Haversham. What does the room look like? What do they do? What does Pip learn about Miss Havisham?
4. Who does Pip meet in the garden and what happens?
5. 'Estella was waiting for me at the gate.' What does she say?
6. After his second visit, Pip goes to Satis House three times every week. What does he tell Miss Havisham about his hopes for the future?

5

1. 'You are getting tall, Pip. What is the name of your brother-in-law, the blacksmith?' Miss Havisham asks.
   (a) Why is this an important question?
   (b) What happens?
   (c) How does Pip feel?
2. 'From that day I lived in fear.'
   What is Pip afraid of?
3. Pip goes to visit Miss Havisham. What does she say? What does he learn about Estella?
4. What happens to Mrs Joe?
5. Who comes to live at the forge?
6. Pip tells this person a secret. What is Pip's secret? What questions does this person ask Pip?
7. Pip believes that Miss Havisham has plans for him. What does he hope and believe?

6

1. Pip has been apprenticed for four years. One evening a stranger comes to find Pip and Joe.
   (a) Why is Pip surprised?
   (b) What does the stranger want?
2. What are Pip's 'great expectations'?

3 'There are two conditions,' the stranger says. What are these conditions?
4 What will happen when Pip is twenty-one? What is going to happen to Pip now?
5 Pip's life is going to change again. How do Biddy and Joe feel about this?
6 Why does Pip walk to the town alone?

7

1 Where does Pip first go when he gets to London? Who does he meet there?
2 Pip is taken to Barnard's Inn.
   (a) Who takes him?
   (b) Who does he meet there?
   (c) Why is Pip surprised to meet this person?
3 Pip's new friend tells him more about Miss Havisham. What does Pip learn about her?
4 Pip wants to become a gentleman.
   (a) Who helps Pip to behave like a gentleman?
   (b) Who is going to educate him as a gentleman?
5 Why does Pip ask Mr Jaggers for more money?
6 Pip goes to Mr Jaggers' house for dinner.
   (a) Who is Bentley Drummle?
   (b) Where had Pip met him?
   (c) What happens between Pip and Bentley Drummle at dinner?
7 'If you want to see strength,' Mr Jaggers said. 'Look at this woman's wrists.' Who is Jaggers speaking about? What does he do?
8 Joe Gargery visits Pip in London.
   (a) Why does he come?
   (b) How does he behave?

8

1 Pip goes to Satis House. How does he feel when he meets Estella again?
2 Miss Havisham talks to Pip about love. What does she say?
3 Why does Pip decide not to visit Joe and Biddy?
4 What does Estella say about herself?
5 Pip and Herbert tell each other their secrets. What are the secrets?

9

1. 'I now come to the time of my life of which I am bitterly ashamed.' Why is Pip ashamed?
2. Why does Estella come to London?
3. How does Estella behave towards Pip?
4. Why does Pip go to visit Joe and Biddy?
5. What happens on Pip's twenty-first birthday?
6. How does Pip help Herbert?
7. 'Who taught me to be proud? Who praised me when I was hard?' Why is Miss Havisham upset by Estella's words?
8. Back in London, Pip is hurt by Estella. How?

10

1. Two years have passed. Herbert is away on business. Who visits Pip one stormy night?
2. Why is Pip horrified by his visitor?
3. Pip goes to see Mr Jaggers. What does Mr Jaggers say when he hears Pip's news?
4. Herbert tells Pip that he must leave England. Why?
5. What story does the strange visitor tell Pip and Herbert?
6. What does Herbert say in his note to Pip?
7. What do Pip and Herbert do next?

11

1. Why are Pip's expectations at an end?
2. Why does Pip go to see Miss Havisham?
3. 'Love is a word I do not understand. I tried to warn you, Pip, but you didn't listen.'
   (a) Who says this to Pip?
   (b) What else does she tell him?
4. When Pip returns to London he finds a message on his door.
   (a) Who wrote the note?
   (b) What does Pip do?
5. Magwitch has some bad news for Pip. What is this news?
6. Herbert has a plan. What is the plan?

7 Pip goes to dinner with Mr Jaggers. What does he discover about Molly?
8 What happens at Satis House when Pip goes to say goodbye to Miss Havisham?
9 In this chapter, what does Pip find out about: Estella, Magwitch and Molly?

12

1 How are Abel Magwitch and Pip going to leave England?
2 What goes wrong?
3 What are Pip's feelings about Magwitch now?
4 What does Magwitch ask Pip to do?
5 Why is Magwitch happy when he dies?

13

1 What happens to Pip's inheritance?
2 Pip becomes very ill.
    (a) Who helps him?
    (b) Where does he go when he gets better?
3 'So my last dream disappeared.'
    (a) What was Pip's dream?
    (b) Why has the dream disappeared?
4 Pip leaves England. How long is he away?
5 When Pip returns to England he goes to the forge. Who does he meet there?
6 Pip goes for a walk.
    (a) Where does he walk to?
    (b) Who does he meet?
    (c) What do they talk about?
7 'And I knew that, this time, we would never, never part.'
   What does Pip mean by these words?

Glossary

SECTION 1
Terms to do with blacksmiths and blacksmithing

apprenticed (page 30)
> when Pip is apprenticed to Joe, he will work for Joe for a number of years and learn to be a blacksmith.

blacksmith (page 8)
> most cities, towns and villages in nineteenth century England had a blacksmith. Blacksmiths made the metal shoes worn by horses and they made and repaired tools and machines made of metal.

file (page 9)
> a metal tool with a rough surface that is used for cutting through metal.

forge (page 11)
> a blacksmith's workshop where the blacksmith heats metals in a fire and makes things.

premium (page 31)
> someone who is going to teach an apprentice must be paid an amount of money, a premium, before the apprentice starts work. Miss Havisham is paying Pip's premium to Joe.

SECTION 2
Terms to do with criminals, lawyers and the law in nineteenth century England

In the nineteenth century, the laws in England were very strict and the prisons were the worst in Europe. People went to prison for many years if they broke the law. Somebody who was accused of committing a crime was put *on trial*. The trial would take place in *court*. A judge would listen to lawyers who would describe what had happened.

If you stole something valuable or killed somebody you could go to prison, or possibly be *sentenced to death by hanging*. If you were found *not guilty*, you were *acquitted* and set free.

In the nineteenth century, criminals could be sent by ship to Australia or New Zealand if they were found guilty of breaking the law. These *convicts* had their hands fastened together by *handcuffs* – iron bands around their wrists – and chains fastened to their legs. They were taken to prison ships called *hulks*. The hulks were old ships that did not move.

They were moored where the River Thames joins the sea. The hulks were dark, dirty and crowded with men, women and children. After they had been in the hulks for a few months, the convicts were put into ships that took them to Australia or New Zealand. In these countries they worked in factories, on farms and in mines. The convicts were never allowed to return to England. They were *transported for life*. If they escaped and returned to England, they would be caught and hanged.

Soldiers and the police stopped people from breaking the law in England in the nineteenth century. There were also officials who made sure that people and goods were not taken out of or brought into England without permission. These officials were called *Customs* men. Customs men lived and worked in all the main towns along the rivers and coast of Britain.

Mr Jaggers is a *criminal lawyer* – he works in the courts where thieves or murderers are tried. Criminals pay him to talk for them in court. These accused people are Mr Jaggers' *clients*. Mr Jaggers is also a lawyer who looks after people's money and business. One of these clients is Pip's *benefactor*. Pip's benefactor is the person who is going to make Pip a very rich man. When he is twenty-one, Pip will become *a man of property*. He will get land, money and houses from his benefactor. Until Pip is twenty-one Mr Jaggers will be Pip's *guardian* and look after Pip's property for him. Mr Jaggers will look after Pip's money and he will decide how much money to give Pip every year as an *allowance*. The benefactor will pay Mr Jaggers to do these things. The benefactor has made two *conditions* – two things Pip must agree with. Pip has to agree with these conditions; if he does not agree he will not become a man of property.

SECTION 3

Adjectives and adverbs

bitter – *a bitter wind* (page 8)
extremely sharp and cold.
bitterly – *bitterly disappointed* (page 31)
very, very disappointed.
faded (page 23)
having little colour. The dresses are dull in colour because they are old.
frosty (page 14)
very cold, so that everything is covered with a thin white coating of ice.

gloomy (page 22)
>dark. The room has very little light coming in through the windows.

icy (page 17)
>the rain is so cold it feels as if it is ice, not water.

misty (page 14)
>covered with a thin layer of cloud near to the ground.

muddy (page 8)
>covered with soft, wet earth. The convict's clothes were wet and dirty.

scornfully (page 22)
>with no respect. The girl feels that Pip is not as important a person as she is.

SECTION 4
Special language in this story

Some of the language in this story is special – for several different reasons. Sometimes characters are not very well educated, like the convict, and they do not speak grammatically. Some characters, like Mrs Joe, like to repeat sayings that were common at this time. These sayings were often clever and a little cruel. Other characters, like Joe, have special sayings of their own.

Ask no questions and you'll be told no lies (page 13)
>this is a saying people use when they are annoyed and don't want to answer a child's questions. It means 'Keep quiet'.

ate (page 11)
>an ungrammatical way of saying 'eaten'.

Curse this iron on my leg (page 15)
>the convict is showing his anger about having the iron on his leg. If you curse something you use angry words about it.

Ever the best of friends (page 38)
>one of Joe's sayings that shows he is kind and that he loves Pip. He means that he and Pip will always be good friends, whatever happens.

God bless you (page 22)
>a common saying which asks God to take care of somebody. Joe is saying this because he wants Pip to be safe and well wherever he goes.

little devil (page 8)
>somebody might say this to a badly behaved child. The convict is saying this to Pip because Pip is making a noise and he wants Pip to be quiet.

look here (page 9)
> the convict is saying – 'Listen to me, pay attention.'

Lord strike me dead if I don't (page 11)
> this is an oath – something you say when you promise to do something. This oath is to make Pip think that something terrible will happen to him if he does not do what the convict wants.

ma'am (page 24)
> a short way of saying 'madam'. Pip knows that this is a polite way of speaking to a lady.

My heart is broken (page 24)
> Miss Havisham is saying that she feels very unhappy because someone has done something terrible to hurt her.

Pip old chap (page 12)
> Joe oftens says this to Pip. He is calling Pip his friend. It is Joe's shy and gentle way of showing that he loves Pip.

I'll play with him (page 22)
> play means 'punish' here. Mrs Joe is making an unpleasant joke using the word 'play'. She has said that Pip must play games at Miss Havisham's. And if Pip doesn't play games, Mrs Joe will punish him.

It's me what's made a gentleman of you (page 60)
> the convict is talking ungrammatically. He should have said 'who' instead of 'what'.

You'd have been in the churchyard long ago, if it hadn't been for me (page 12)
> Mrs Joe is angry again. She is saying that Pip would have been dead if she had not looked after him.

SECTION 5
General

admired (page 16)
> liked very much. Mr Pumblechook thought that Mrs Joe was a very good person.

adopted (page 40)
> Estella did not have anyone to look after her. Miss Havisham went to court and became Estella's parent by law. She brought Estella up as her daughter.

bow (page 16)
> a polite way of saying hello to somebody by bending your head and body forwards.

common (page 24)
   Estella is being rude about Pip. She is saying that he is from a lower class than she is. Estella wears fine clothes and lives in a big house. Pip wears rough working clothes and lives at the forge. Estella is saying that Pip is not as good a person as she is.

debt – *get into debt* (page 40)
   spend all your money, so you have to borrow more money from somebody else.

ditch (page 14)
   a narrow channel that is dug between fields or at the side of a road to hold water.

dressing gown (page 46)
   a kind of loose coat that Pip is wearing over his indoor clothes. Pip is dressed like a fashionable young man and Joe has never seen Pip dressed like this before. (Nowadays we wear dressing gowns over our nightclothes.)

dressing room (page 23)
   a room, usually next to a bedroom, where somebody gets dressed or changes their clothes.

elegant (page 48)
   very well-dressed and fashionable.

entrap (page 57)
   trick somebody. Estella is making these young men believe that she likes them, but she really does not care about them.

flags – *played with flags . . . and waved our swords* (page 27)
   a flag is a piece of cloth that is attached to a pole. A sword is a long sharp knife that is used for fighting. Pip is telling lies about playing with these things.

fortune – *good fortune* (page 38)
   your fortune is what happens to you in your life. Good fortune is good luck. Sometimes fortune means a lot of money.

growled (page 8)
   spoke in a low, angry voice.

in torment (page 49)
   feeling unhappy or ill because something is making you very upset.

invalid (page 51)
   a person who is ill and will always be ill.

knitting (page 67)
   making something out of wool using two long needles.

limping (page 9)
: walking unevenly. Having difficulty in walking because there is something wrong with your foot or leg.

lost (page 32)
: you lose a person if you spend a lot of time with them and care about them, and then you don't see them any more.

moored (page 13)
: a ship that is fastened to the land by a rope is moored.

muttered (page 9)
: the convict is talking very quietly to himself.

Old Fort (page 11)
: a fort is a strong building where soldiers live. Forts were built to protect a town or a country from enemies. The Old Fort is a fort on the marshes that is not used any more.

paddle steamer (page 74)
: a paddle steamer is a large ship which has large wheels at either side to move it through the water.

partner (page 54)
: a person who owns part of a business.

pony cart (page 19)
: a small wooden vehicle with two wheels that is pulled along by a pony.

river – *mouth of the river* (page 68)
: the river is the River Thames which flows through London. Its mouth is where the river flows out to join the sea.

row (page 68)
: move a boat through the water by using oars.

tide – *high tide* (page 74)
: near to the sea, the level of water in the River Thames rises and falls twice a day like the sea does. High tide is when there is the most water in the river. A big ship has to move along the river at high tide because at low tide there will not be enough water for it to float.

upside down (page 9)
: the man has picked Pip up and has turned him over, so Pip's feet are in the air and his head is near the ground.

wedding veil (page 23)
: a piece of thin, soft, white cloth that a bride wears on her head when she is wearing her wedding dress.

Macmillan Education Limited
4 Crinan Street
London N1 9XW

Companies and representatives throughout the world

Macmillan Readers Upper Level Great Expectations
ISBN: 978-1-035-15132-5
Macmillan Readers Upper Level Great Expectations with eBook and Resources
ISBN: 978-1-035-15135-6

This is a retold version by Florence Bell of the original work by Charles Dickens.
Text © Florence Bell 1993, 2002, 2005, 2024
Design and illustration © Macmillan Education Limited 2002, 2005, 2024

First published 1993
This edition published 2024

All rights reserved. No part of this publication may be reproduced, stored in a retrieval system, or transmitted in any form or by any means, electronic, mechanical, photocopying, recording, or otherwise, without the prior written permission of the publishers.

Illustrated by Kay Dixey
Cover illustration by Ashley Pierce

Printed and bound by CPI Group (UK) Ltd, Croydon, CR0 4YY
POD 2026